THE M WORD

THE

M

WORD

WRITERS ON SAME-SEX MARRIAGE

Edited by Kathy Pories

ALGONQUIN BOOKS OF CHAPEL HILL

2004

Published by
ALGONQUIN BOOKS OF CHAPEL HILL
Post Office Box 2225
Chapel Hill, North Carolina 27515-2225

a division of
Workman Publishing
708 Broadway
New York, New York 10003

"My Amendment" by George Saunders first appeared in the *New Yorker*.
"Double Standards" by Dan Savage first appeared on Salon.com.

Library of Congress Cataloging-in-Publication Data
The M word : writers on same-sex marriage /
edited by Kathy Pories.—1st ed.
    p. cm.
 ISBN 1-56512-454-5
 1. Same-sex marriage.   I. Pories, Kathy, 1961–
HQ1033.M6 2004
306.84'8—dc22   2004054571

10 9 8 7 6 5 4 3 2 1
First Edition

CONTENTS

The editor would like to thank all the writers who made time to contribute to this anthology, as well as those at Algonquin who made this happen with lightning speed and precision—and kept their patience with me: Brunson Hoole, Sally Cassady Lyon, and Anne Winslow.

PREFACE

WHEN I WAS GROWING UP in a suburb of Cleveland in the seventies, my parents weren't the only ones to divorce. We were apparently on the crest of a wave; more of my friends' parents were divorced, on their way to a divorce, or in a sad facade of a marriage maintained for social reasons than were happily married. At the time, gay marriage was, in my small world at least, nowhere on the horizon. Queer was a word we used constantly to refer to anything out of the ordinary; and when we called someone gay, it was a boy who seemed somewhat feminine. That was about the limit of our understanding.

This past spring, as gay couples began to insist on their right to marry, I could open the Raleigh paper nearly any morning and find, along with the occasional supportive letter, one furious or frightened letter after another detailing the ways in which gay marriage was a threat to the institution of marriage, would unravel this sacred commitment eventually, would undo what little stability we had left in our culture. It wasn't exclusive to letters to the editor, of course; I read serious editorials explaining to me why I should not let this happen, especially if I cared about the future of our children. Children who might be raised in a household of an abnormal couple, two women, or (worse) two men.

Suffice it to say that no one's gayness had anything to do with my parents' divorce or the crumbling marriages all around us back in the seventies. And when my own marriage fell apart more recently, it was for numerous reasons: incompatibility, immaturity, inability to face the facts of what was happening between us, unwillingness to change what had become a whole set of bad behaviors; maybe, too, finally and most important, not enough love to ride it all out. Or you might've just said we weren't committed enough to each other. We'd gone to a justice of the peace, we were considered married by law by the state, we were accompanied by two of our closest friends as witnesses, and later we had a party where we were surrounded by family and friends to cement the union. We exchanged rings. We made vows. We got money, we got presents, we bought furniture.

When the marriage became irreparable in both of our minds and when we knew we could no longer be in the same house together, the state of North Carolina insisted that we be separated for one year before our divorce could become final. In case we changed our minds and decided to reunite.

None of those rituals, nor the state's mandatory one-year separation that would presumably urge us to try it all over again, determined the course of our marriage and its eventual decline.

Nor did any gay marriage or gay union happening in our vicinity, or any gay couple anywhere in the country, have an effect on what occurred between us. Next door lived a lesbian couple who'd long ago given up trying to legally adopt their daughter. They had been together for twenty-five years. Down the street was another lesbian couple with a daughter. The two girls played together, the couples lived their lives and worked their jobs and had seasonal potluck parties to which we were invited, year after year. At Christmas, they showed up at our door caroling. I don't think I could find any reason under the sun to hold them responsible for what happened in our house, unless by comparison they demonstrated what happier houses looked like.

Maybe I was missing something this spring as I read the papers, but I was truly perplexed as to why people were so insistent on erecting roadblocks between two people who'd decided to commit themselves to each other as best they could—not because society expected them to marry at a certain age, or because they felt an urgent need to have children and carry on the family name, or, oops, they were expecting a child and needed to make it legitimate, but because—at the risk of sounding redundant—they wanted to commit themselves to each other.

The more I read the paper, the more frustrated I became; everyone was writing letters about it, but in short takes, invoking slippery-slope arguments, all of which felt oddly out of balance to the issue at hand. It wasn't that I wanted to read polemics about the right to gay marriage; I wanted to read writers considering it thoughtfully, explaining to me the nuances of this debate, why it might feel like such a threat to some, why it might be downright cruel to prevent others from marrying, and why many gay people looking around themselves at the poor record of heterosexual marriages were wary of marriage altogether. I guess I wanted to understand what my marriage—and unmarriage—had to do with theirs. And just what it was that "they" were doing to the institution of the American family.

That's all I wanted to read when I contacted writers, gay and straight, asking for their thoughts on same-sex marriage. But as you'll see, I got so much more.

—Kathy Pories

THE M WORD

Jamie's Wedding

BY WENDY BRENNER

I NEVER HAD STRONG FEELINGS, or any feelings, about marriage laws. As a perennially single straight woman, I didn't have to. It struck me as a little crazy that people got so bent out of shape over rules for what was essentially a game of pretend, Pee-Wee Herman walking down the aisle with the bowl of fruit salad: *If you love fruit salad so much, why don't you marry it?*

Still, I cried when my friend Jamie asked me to give him away—suddenly, it was personal. He and his boyfriend, Bradley, were planning a formal ceremony in a chapel at the edge of a lake in the lushly overgrown Florida college town that was my favorite place in the world: where I had lived through most of my twenties, where I figured out I could be a writer. Jamie actually wanted me to walk him down the aisle and speak on his behalf. Nobody, gay or straight, had ever asked me to do anything of the kind. My thirties were going swiftly by, no wedding of my own in sight. It had come to my attention that I wasn't having children. Previously normal acquaintances went around saying soap-opera sentences like, "It's the hardest thing you'll ever do, but also the most rewarding." Nobody was suggesting I *needed* to get married to be happy (besides every person on TV), but still, I felt defensive. My work, teaching and writing, had taken up most of my adult life—so it felt like vindication that Jamie, my former student, thought of me as family. *I can't tell you what this means to me,* I told him.

He was family to me, too, the little brother I never had. He'd shown up in my fiction-writing class in that lush Florida town ten years ago, when I was a graduate teaching assistant, growing poorer and more worried every day, wondering if I'd ever write a book that got published, whether my life was ever going to arrive, or if it was languishing out there in the world somewhere, unclaimed, in the Lost & Found of lives. Jamie appeared just in time, as angels do. He was nineteen, the youngest in the class and the only gay person, a cheerful, wholesome, fresh-faced blond in a roomful of chain-smoking tough guys who modeled themselves after Charles Bukowski or Kurt Cobain, who had killed himself a few months before. Unfazed and irrepressible, Jamie wrote twice as much and as fast as everyone else, stylish, funny, openly sentimental stories whose characters were irreverent and full of wonder by turns. In class, he rolled his eyes when people spoke, he made passionate allies and enemies, he acted like everything mattered, he never got bored. He seemed familiar to me—the way hope might feel to someone who hadn't had any for a while. My other friends were mostly in the same boat as myself, struggling young writers and artists afraid of the future. Jamie didn't seem afraid of anything. He reminded me why I loved my job, and my life.

He was paying his own tuition working at the kind of "real" jobs I'd always hoped to avoid—bank teller, insurance customer service rep, assistant manager of a Winn-Dixie—but he seemed no worse for wear, the forty-hour weeks never denting his stellar grade point average or frenetic social life. He had a million friends, yet he also was a good friend, two characteristics that don't always go together.

When I had to fly to New York for a job interview, it was Jamie who drove me ninety miles to the airport before dawn, singing along to "I'm Too Sexy" on the radio and shimmying so hard in his seat that the car shook. He taught me how to make his mother's famous Tennessee honey-buttermilk biscuits while a melancholy techno dance track called "Children" played over and over on repeat for three hours, neither of us getting sick of it. I spent long Sunday afternoons hanging out at his apartment grading papers while he practiced making various desserts, a brief, unsuccessful obsession. I still have a photo of him furiously, hilariously *imitating* a piece of cake, a particularly maddening recipe that slumped at the slightest touch of a fork.

He talked a lot about his happy Southern childhood, his close-knit, fiercely loyal family. Even now that he was on his own, his parents still dropped everything and drove hundreds of miles to the rescue if they ever thought he was in trouble. He didn't share their Baptist faith, yet he had never felt the need to rebel against it—he wanted the same things they had: lasting love, a stable home, maybe even kids. When he came out to them, in the fall of his senior year of college, they seemed to adjust with astonishing speed and grace, even going so far as to invite his boyfriend of the moment home for Christmas. I had Christmas dinner with them, too, one year; his mother sewed a stocking with my name on it. I thought I was beginning to understand where Jamie got his resilience and optimism and endless energy. His was the family I'd always wished for.

My own, back in Chicago, was the opposite in every way: secular, distant, violent. So difficult was I as a child, my mother testified, that sometimes she had to hit me until her hand hurt. I was a fighter by nature, which made things worse. Often I went to school in tears; I remember a boy at the bus stop one morning asking me what was wrong, and realizing with sudden shame from his kind but confused expression that not everyone had screaming fights over breakfast. After I moved away to Florida for graduate school I only saw them every few years or so, by some civil, unspoken arrangement, a kind of truce. Our phone calls were polite but infrequent; they didn't want to hear too much about my life, didn't ask about my work or friends or boyfriends. And, to be fair, neither did I take any interest in their bird-watching and butterfly-collecting, postretirement passions that led them through jungles and deserts on nearly every continent—though they never quite got around to visiting me in Florida. We were more like distant acquaintances than family, and conversely, over the years, my friends more and more became my relatives.

As if Jamie had heralded it, my life did arrive not long after we met. My first book got published and I landed a permanent teaching job in a North Carolina beach town. It was not only the ocean that attracted me, but the wildly social young community of faculty and graduate students, the invitations to potlucks and barbecues and karaoke nights that came over my email months before I even moved there. I had turned down a better-paying job, in fact, at a private university where the people seemed polite but remote; the head of the English department, in an attempt to lure me, said that what it really came down to was whether I wanted to teach students like theirs, or "state-school students" in North Carolina. Jamie was a state-school student, I thought. There was no contest. In North Carolina I felt I'd finally found a home, or made one, in the world.

Jamie stayed in Florida, getting promotions and raises and spending his weekends driving all over the state with carloads of friends, hitting clubs and raves and Disney Gay Days, dancing on loudspeakers in Miami and crashing private parties in Tampa and getting chased out of Orlando by someone's jealous boyfriend, sometimes all in the same night. *The entire city of Tallahassee now hates us,* he'd announce proudly, recounting his latest adventure. But he wasn't just out for thrills. He got phone numbers, chased guys and made them chase him, waited for calls and dates as eagerly as any teenager. Every boy he met or danced with or drunkenly kissed, however fleetingly, might turn out to be The One, the love of his life.

In someone else this gushiness might have seemed naïve, but Jamie was a pragmatist, more able than anyone I knew to reconcile romance with reality. He paid his own bills, knew how to be alone, but also knew how to be with someone, how to sleep in the same bed and do laundry and dishes together and drive each other crazy occasionally but get over it. Unlike me, he tended to see imperfections, his own and those of his boyfriends, as amusing, not catastrophic.

We had long telephone conversations about destiny and soulmates, both of which we stubbornly believed in, against our better judgment. He dated all different kinds of guys, he kept an open mind, he let himself get hurt, he kept trying. I tried to remind him to keep the faith, as he'd always reminded me. *It's going to be hard to find someone who's strong enough for you,* I told him countless times. Most men twice his age still hadn't figured out what they wanted. I suspected there were many more confused and damaged people out there, like myself, than healthy, confident ones like Jamie. He moved in with guys a few times, but they were never quite as loyal as he, or as ambitious, or as fun. Weak men seemed to seek him out, guys who couldn't quite support themselves, or couldn't make their own friends. For a few months with one boyfriend Jamie wore a gold wedding band—his first day at a new bank job, I remember, a coworker asked his wife's name, to which he answered without missing a beat, "Tabitha"—but that relationship, too, turned out to be short-lived.

I don't remember the first time he told me about Bradley. Unlike his previous boyfriends, who tended to explode into his life in fireworks displays of signs and omens and fateful coincidences, Bradley arrived without drama. The only irony, a kind of *It's a Wonderful Life* twist, was that Jamie, having exhausted the state of Florida, had for the past couple of years resorted to meeting men on-line, resulting in complicated, disappointing long-distance entanglements—while Bradley was living right there in Gainesville all along. He was a hairdresser at the hippest salon in town; he went to all the same clubs and parties as Jamie. He had a long-term, loyal clientele, and, like Jamie, a million friends of all ages, gay and straight. The only miracle was that they hadn't met sooner.

They lived together two or three years before they decided to get married. From the very beginning, though, their relationship always reminded me of Rilke's definition of love, *two solitudes [that] protect and border and salute each other*—something I still held out hope of finding for myself someday.

I BRAGGED TO ANYONE who would listen: *I'm walking him down the aisle, actually giving him away!* I was no better than my friends, the Smug Marrieds, passing around their ultrasound pictures. Secretly, I even thought I was *ahead* of them, for once—none of them would be walking anyone down the aisle for years. In a socially acceptable way, I was finally getting to tell the world, "Look, my life is meaningful, too."

Only of course it wasn't socially acceptable. The salesgirls at Nine West, who a moment earlier had been complimenting the dress I'd just bought, suddenly averted their eyes when I mentioned that it was a gay wedding. When I told the woman who'd cut my hair for six years—whom I considered a friend, and who by virtue of her profession, I thought, could not possibly have a problem with gays—she smirked and said, "So, are you going to wear a tuxedo?"

These reactions shouldn't have surprised me, yet somehow they did. They gave me, I knew, just the tiniest taste of what Jamie's life was like, or Bradley's, or a million other people's. I was beginning to feel zealous about a cause in which I hadn't thought I had any stake.

More than ever, I wanted my own small part in the ceremony to be perfect, to do justice to the magnitude and legitimacy of the occasion. I felt an overwhelming responsibility to honor Jamie's family, all of whom planned to attend. I had always been a little awed and intimidated by "real" families, as if it were somehow my own fault that I didn't have one, and I wondered if Jamie's parents knew how much he attributed to them: his strength of character, his optimism, his work ethic, his faith in love. Composing something to read at the ceremony was harder than I expected—he couldn't have found someone who knew less about this particular convention. Everything I wrote came out sounding like a recommendation letter: *I am confident he will succeed . . .* Finally I asked my married friends for help, and their advice surprised me. *You can't be too emotional or sentimental,* they said. In twenty years of studying and teaching writing, I had never heard or given that suggestion.

In the end, I tried to list the things Jamie had taught me, or reminded me, when I most needed reminding: To believe in miracles. To approach life with both reverence and irreverence—that those two approaches are not mutually exclusive. To remember that love can't be broken by one wrong word or one wrong move. I tried to describe Jamie's glow, his irrepressibility, his gift for making friends with warp speed wherever he went, the way he loved people's complications and absurdities and imperfections. I told how he had never lost faith, never doubted he'd recognize his soulmate when that person arrived—and he had. I cried every time I reread it, which I figured was a good sign.

Then a few weeks before the wedding, Jamie sent me an email: *My mom and dad have decided they are not coming to the ceremony due to their religious beliefs. I have to say I am not surprised—I would have been more surprised if they came. I am disappointed and in a way, relieved, because I know I would have worried the whole time if they were uncomfortable. My mom sent me a letter—which I knew what it was before I even opened it. I have not responded yet. I know they probably think I am pissed off which I am totally not. So regardless, it will still be a beautiful day and I will have plenty of other family (i.e., you) there.*

THE DAY WAS BEAUTIFUL, in the way only a Florida day can be. The wedding began at sunset, the sky turning the unlikely hues of old hand-colored postcards, Spanish moss dripping down from live oaks in the still air over Lake Alice, all of this visible through the tall, skinny glass walls of the chapel, framed by yellow pine and Florida cypress and copper. Every seat was filled, and because of the space limit a hundred more guests were invited to the reception only; between the two of them, Jamie and Bradley seemed to know every person in town. As I walked Jamie down the aisle, our arms linked, the kindness in the faces turned to watch us was overwhelming. In the front pew sat Bradley's parents, his brother and sister-in-law and nephew, Jamie's sister, and my friend Bekki, who had made the nine-hour drive from North Carolina for the occasion. A classical guitarist played Pachelbel's Canon in D, then "Autumn Leaves." A vocalist sang Christine McVie's "Songbird," so beautiful it was nearly sadistic: the silence when the music stopped was thick with choked-back emotion.

A minister Bradley knew through his salon was officiating, a platinum-blond, beatific-faced woman who looked a bit like a New-Age Barbara Mandrell, dressed in sparkly white. The ceremony was not New Age-y, however, but formal and traditional, including a blessing of the rings and many references to the Bible, the Divine, and angels (in his vows, Bradley said he had not believed in them until he met Jamie). On the program was printed an epigraph from Tolstoy: *All, everything that I understand, I understand only because I love.* There were no political references, nothing to mark the occasion as anything other than "normal"—except a single, sobering note, when the minister called for a moment of silence "for those who cannot be with us today, whether lost through death or through fear."

I thought of Jamie's parents. "They've come so far," his sister had told me, "but they just couldn't do this last thing." She'd been talking to them on the phone every night, filling them in on the details about the ceremony and the plans for the honeymoon, an elaborately mapped-out road trip that would loop the couple through Mississippi and Texas and Colorado. "Dad is so excited about the honeymoon," she said, "I think he wants to go with them."

Two hundred people packed into a museum of Florida antiques and artifacts in the town's oldest residence for the wedding reception, a lavish buffet dinner and dancing to both a live band and a DJ. As the party wound down, I stood on the porch with Bekki under the stars and palm fronds, inhaling the ineffably calming swampy night air, trying to tell her what this place meant to me—but it was both impossible and unnecessary: she already knew. She'd read my books, knew that every story I wrote took place here, the setting in which I could most easily imagine people being transformed, as I had been. Her presence here, in fact, felt a little magical, as if she were an emissary from my present life, visiting my past with me. It was what we all wanted but only rarely got, I thought—a witness. It was why all those children's books about runaway horses and dogs who'd lost their owners were so sad—the animals could never explain to anyone what had happened to them, but were forced to carry their histories and memories mutely around, their hearts breaking.

There was no ceremony invented for this moment. No ritual when I moved to North Carolina, or piece of paper to certify: *You are finally home.* When I came to realize, over a period of years, that my friends had become my family, there was no way to notarize that fact, to make it official. I thought of something Jamie said in his vows: *We always say life is about the journey, not the destination. Well, today, for once, it's about the destination.*

THREE WEEKS AFTER the wedding I was diagnosed with cancer. My parents didn't fly in for my surgery, or during the months that followed. "We'll come later, when you're feeling better," my father said, but they never did. Instead they went to Paris for a weekend, something to do with Frequent Flier miles, using them up or getting new ones, and then they went bird-watching in Belize. This did not surprise me— yet I was surprised by how much it still hurt, after so many years, and how it still made me feel so unaccountably ashamed. I had thought I was used to it. People who didn't know me well asked if my family was coming, then looked pained or pitying when I answered.

My friends rallied, as they always have. They got my groceries and prescriptions, waited with me for doctors to call, stayed with me at night if I wanted or slept with their cell phones turned on if I didn't, surrounded me with food and flowers and people and prayers. I was never alone. If I thought too much about my parents, I'd remind myself how lucky I was to have dozens of people who loved me, instead of just two. A card came from my colleagues and students at school, signed *From your Creative Writing family.*

In the hospital, I kept a photo I'd snapped at the wedding on my bedside table, Jamie embracing Bradley's seven-year-old nephew, who'd stolen the show as ring bearer. They beamed out in their matching, satiny vests and ties, their faces radiating light and love, Jamie's glow actually captured, for once, on film. It's the kind of photo you can't look at without smiling—none of the seemingly hundreds of nurses and doctors who came through my room that week walked by it without stopping for a second look, almost hungrily, a moment out of their day to focus on something other than suffering. *My friend Jamie's gay wedding,* I told anyone who asked, and for once nobody frowned or smirked or turned away, although I doubted the medical community was any more liberal than the rest of the population. Maybe they were just being polite to a cancer patient, I thought. Or maybe people who saw death every day just had a better sense of what was important.

My Amendment

BY GEORGE SAUNDERS

As an obscure, middle-aged, heterosexual short-story writer, I am often asked, George, do you have any feelings about Same-Sex Marriage?

To which I answer, Actually, yes, I do.

Like any sane person, I am against Same-Sex Marriage, and in favor of a constitutional amendment to ban it.

To tell the truth, I feel that, in the interest of moral rigor, it is necessary for us to go a step further, which is why I would like to propose a supplementary constitutional amendment.

In the town where I live, I have frequently observed a phenomenon I have come to think of as Samish-Sex Marriage. Take, for example, K, a male friend of mine, of slight build, with a ponytail. K is married to S, a tall, stocky female with extremely short hair, almost a crewcut. Often, while watching K play with his own ponytail as S towers over him,

I have wondered, Isn't it odd that this somewhat effeminate man should be married to this somewhat masculine woman? Is K not, on some level, imperfectly expressing a slight latent desire to be married to a man? And is not S, on some level, imperfectly expressing a slight latent desire to be married to a woman?

Then I ask myself, Is this truly what God had in mind?

Take the case of L, a female friend with a deep, booming voice. I have often found myself looking askance at her husband, H. Though H is basically pretty masculine, having neither a ponytail nor a tight feminine derrière like K, still I wonder: H, when you are having marital relations with L, and she calls out your name in that deep, booming, nearly male voice, and you continue having marital relations with her (i.e., you are not "turned off"), does this not imply that you, H, are, in fact, still "turned on"? And doesn't this indicate that, on some level, you, H, have a slight latent desire to make love to a man?

Or consider the case of T, a male friend with an extremely small penis. (We attend the same gym.) He is married to O, an average-looking woman who knows how to fix cars. I wonder about O. How does she know so much about cars? Is she not, by tolerating this non-car-fixing, short-penised friend of mine, indicating that, on some level, she wouldn't mind being married to a woman, and is therefore, perhaps, a tiny bit functionally gay?

And what about T? Doesn't the fact that T can stand there in the shower room at our gym, confidently towelling off his tiny unit, while O is at home changing their spark-plugs with alacrity, indicate that it is only a short stroll down a slippery slope before he is completely happy being the "girl" in their relationship, from which it is only a small fey hop down the same slope before T is happily married to another man, perhaps my car mechanic, a handsome Portuguese fellow I shall refer to as J?

Because my feeling is, when God made man and woman He had something very specific in mind. It goes without saying that He did not want men marrying men, or women marrying women, but also what He did not want, in my view, was feminine men marrying masculine women.

Which is why I developed my Manly Scale of Absolute Gender.

Using my Scale, which assigns numerical values according to a set of masculine and feminine characteristics, it is now easy to determine how Manly a man is and how Fem a woman is, and therefore how close to a Samish-Sex Marriage a given marriage is.

Here's how it works. Say we determine that a man is an 8 on the Manly Scale, with 10 being the most Manly of all and o basically a Neuter. And say we determine that his fiancée is a –6 on the Manly Scale, with a –10 being the most Fem of all. Calculating the difference between the man's rating and the woman's rating—the Gender Differential—we see that this proposed union is not, in fact, a Samish-Sex Marriage, which I have defined as "any marriage for which the Gender Differential is less than or equal to 10 points."

Friends whom I have identified as being in Samish-Sex Marriages often ask me, George, given that we have scored poorly, what exactly would you have us do about it?

Well, one solution I have proposed is divorce—divorce followed by remarriage to a more suitable partner. K, for example, could marry a voluptuous high-voiced N.F.L. cheerleader, who would more than offset his tight feminine derrière, while his ex-wife, S, might choose to become involved with a lumberjack with very large arms, thereby neutralizing her thick calves and faint mustache.

Another, and of course preferable, solution would be to repair the existing marriage, converting from a Samish-Sex Marriage to a healthy Normal Marriage, by having the feminine man become more masculine and/or the masculine woman become more feminine.

Often, when I propose this, my friends become surly. How dare I, they ask. What business is it of mine? Do I think it is easy to change in such a profound way?

To which I say, It is not easy to change, but it is possible. I know, because I have done it.

When young, I had a tendency to speak too quickly, while gesturing too much with my hands. Also, my opinions were unfirm. I was constantly contradicting myself in that fast voice, while gesturing like a girl. Also, I cried often. Things seemed so sad. I had long blond hair, and liked it. My hair was layered and fell down across my shoulders, and, I admit it, I would sometimes slow down when passing a shop-window to look at it, to look at my hair! I had a strange constant feeling of being happy to be alive. This feeling of infinite possibility sometimes caused me to laugh when alone, or even, on occasion, to literally skip down the street, before pausing in front of a shopwindow and giving my beautiful hair a cavalier toss.

To tell the truth, I do not think I would have scored very high on my Manly Scale, if the Scale had been invented at that time, by me. I suspect I would have scored so Fem on the test that I would have been prohibited from marrying my wife, P, the love of my life. And I think, somewhere in my heart, I knew that.

I knew I was too Fem.

So what did I do about it? Did I complain? Did I whine? Did I expect activist judges to step in on my behalf, manipulating the system to accommodate my peculiarity?

No, I did not.

What I did was I changed. I undertook what I like to think of as a classic American project of self-improvement. I made videos of myself talking, and studied these, and in time succeeded in training myself to speak more slowly, while almost never moving my hands. Now, if you ever meet me, you will observe that I always speak in an extremely slow and manly and almost painfully deliberate way, with my hands either driven deep into my pockets or held stock-still at the ends of my arms, which are bent slightly at the elbows, as if I were ready to respond to the slightest provocation by punching you in the face. As for my opinions, they are very firm. I rarely change them. When I feel like skipping, I absolutely do not skip. As for my long beautiful hair—well, I am lucky, in that I am rapidly going bald. Every month, when I recalculate my ranking on the Manly Scale, I find myself becoming more and more Manly, as my hair gets thinner and my girth increases, thickening my once lithe, almost girlish physique, thus insuring the continuing morality and legality of my marriage to P.

My point is simply this: If I was able to effect these tremendous positive changes in my life, to avoid finding myself in the moral/legal quagmire of a Samish-Sex Marriage, why can't K, S, L, H, T, and O do the same?

I implore any of my readers who find themselves in a Samish-Sex Marriage: Change. If you are a feminine man, become more manly. If you are a masculine woman, become more feminine. If you are a woman and are thick-necked or lumbering, or have ever had the slightest feeling of attraction to a man who is somewhat pale and fey, deny these feelings and, in a spirit of self-correction, try to become more thin-necked and light-footed, while, if you find it helpful, watching videos of naked masculine men, to sort of retrain yourself in the proper mode of attraction. If you are a man and, upon seeing a thick-waisted, athletic young woman walking with a quasi-mannish gait through your local grocery, you imagine yourself in a passionate embrace with her, in your car, a car that is parked just outside, and which is suddenly, in your imagination, full of the smell of her fresh young breath—well, stop thinking that! Are you a man or not?

I, for one, am sick and tired of this creeping national tendency to let certain types of people take advantage of our national good nature by marrying individuals who are essentially of their own gender. If this trend continues, before long our towns and cities will be full of people like K, S, L, H, T, and O, people "asserting their rights" by dating, falling in love with, marrying, and spending the rest of their lives with whomever they please.

I, for one, am not about to stand by and let that happen.

Because then what will we have? A nation ruled by the anarchy of unconstrained desire. A nation of willful human hearts, each lurching this way and that and reaching out for whatever it spontaneously desires, trying desperately to find some comforting temporary shred of warmth in a mostly cold world, totally unconcerned about the external form in which that other, long-desired heart is embodied.

That is not the kind of world in which I wish to live.

I, for one, intend to become ever more firmly male, enjoying my golden years, while watching P become ever more female, each of us vigilant for any hint of ambiguity in the other.

And as our children grow, should they begin to show the slightest hint of some lingering residue of the opposite gender, P and I will lovingly pull them aside and list all the particulars by which we were able to identify their unintentional deficiency.

Then, together, we will devise a suitable correction.

And, in this way, the race will go on.

Notes toward an Opinion on Gay Marriage

BY DAVID LEAVITT

No matter what decision a person makes,
whether to get married or to remain single, he is
always bound to regret it.
—FRANZ LISZT

I.

SPRING, AND SUDDENLY it seems that everywhere I turn, men I am close to are divorcing their wives. Colleagues, friends, my brother. All are in their early fifties. One says, "Fifty-one. A good age for divorce." Another has left his wife for one of her closest friends. "I'm a bad demographic," he tells me, bewilderment in his voice. "I never thought I'd be a bad demographic."

Some days he talks about the mediation. He talks about the division of property in terms of red apples and green apples: "If I bring three red apples to the marriage and she brings five green apples, the point is, we have eight apples." But on better days—days when he has seen his girlfriend— he talks about hope. He uses the word "possibility." He uses the word "future."

Only when I ask him, "If things don't work out with your girlfriend, would you consider returning to your wife?" he hesitates a moment and then says, "No. Absolutely not."

But he does hesitate.

2.

MARK AND I have lived together for almost thirteen years. We own, jointly, a house and a car. We have two joint bank accounts. We have a dog. For the first five years we kept our books and CDs separate, but then we put them together, and they have been together ever since.

One thing we do not have is a shared health insurance policy, because (as of this writing) the university at which I teach has chosen not to extend benefits to domestic partners. And—it goes without saying—we cannot marry.

Would we, if we could? When asked, we usually answer that if we were straight, we'd be like one of those couples who met in the sixties, when marriage was out of fashion, and then just never bothered to tie the knot.

Still, in private at least, we refer to our relationship, almost automatically, as a marriage.

3.

DIVORCE HASN'T BEEN such a feature in my life since the early seventies, when it seemed that every couple in the world —my parents' friends, my friends' parents—was getting divorced. My parents were the exception. They stayed together, for better or worse, until my mother died. At night my mother knitted, while reading new novels by feminist writers, most of which had heroines who had just left or been left by their husbands.

A memory that for some reason has stuck with me: Diane Briglia sitting alone in the cafeteria in eighth grade, reading *The Kids' Guide to Divorce*. I couldn't believe she was doing it in public. That year most of us were reading *Love Story* or *The Exorcist*.

I felt sorry for Diane Briglia. I thought, "That poor thing." Because, of course, it seemed inconceivable to me that *my* parents would ever divorce. And if they did, they would certainly never have given me a book called *The Kids' Guide to Divorce*. And I certainly would never have read it in the cafeteria, in front of everyone, the way Diane Briglia did, her face steely with resolve and perhaps defiance.

That afternoon, when I got home, I listened to my favorite record album of the moment, which was Joni Mitchell's *Blue*. I listened to Joni singing "My Old Man" about how we don't need no piece of paper from City Hall keeping us tied and true.

"*Tied* and true." Clever, that Joni.

A few years later my parents' marriage came to a point of crisis. They reconciled—perhaps because my mother was sick. Now my brother and I wonder if they would have been happier if they *had* divorced. At the time, my mother claimed she couldn't have survived without my father. Perhaps. But today we think that she would not just have survived, but thrived.

As for us, we wonder if indeed we would have suffered more from their separating (as we feared then) than we did from their staying together (as we know now).

• • •

4.

E. M. FORSTER WAS determined that his novel *Maurice* should have a happy ending. "I shouldn't have bothered to write otherwise," he later reflected. "I was determined that in fiction anyway two men should fall in love and remain in it for the ever and ever that fiction allows . . ." So at the end of the novel, Maurice and Alec Scudder disappear into "the greenwood," to pass the rest of their years together. Away from society. Beyond even the author's reach.

Forster never could figure out what to say about that "ever and ever." Thus we never see Maurice and Alec in middle age or beyond: cooking, gardening, squabbling about bills. An epilogue in which Maurice's sister encounters "two woodcutters some years later . . . gave universal dissatisfaction" and was thrown away.

Lytton Strachey, for one, was unsatisfied with the ending as it stood: "I should be inclined to diagnose Maurice's state as simply lust and sentiment," he wrote to Forster, "—a very wobbly affair; I should have prophesied a rupture after 6 months—chiefly as a result of lack of common interests owing to class differences—I believe even such a simple-minded fellow as Maurice would have felt this—"

Is there a story to be written here? A novel? *Two Wood-cutters, Some Years Later* . . . The question it would answer—a question directed perhaps at Lytton Strachey—is: "Why not?"

5.

MOST OF MY favorite novels are about marriages. Fantastic, fraught, larger-than-life, disputatious marriages. These are grandiose edifices, but structurally unstable. You walk into them at your own risk. Usually in these novels the hero or narrator is a befuddled male friend who, if not homosexual, is at least a bachelor, or if not a bachelor, then at least the victim of a shrewish wife. The Ashburnhams of Ford Madox Ford's *The Good Soldier*, wildly unhappy and utterly proper, we learn about from poor John Dowell, with whose wife Edward Ashburnham is having an affair. The bachelor Alwyn Tower, whose brother will end up marrying his own putative amour, Alexandra Henry, tells us the story of the Cullens and their falcon in Glenway Wescott's *The Pilgrim Hawk*. Then there are the bachelor heroes of Iris Murdoch's novels: Charles Arrowby of *The Sea, The Sea*, who says, "What suits me best is the drama of separation, of looking forward to assignations and rendezvous. I cannot prefer the awful eternal presence of marriage to the magic of meetings and partings." Or Bradley Pearson from *The Black Prince*, who observes the volatile marriage of his friends Arnold and Rachel Baffin and reflects: "What a mystery marriage was. What a strange and violent world, the world of matrimony. I was glad to be outside it." Marriage stands at the red-hot center of these novels, yet the perspective of the storyteller is off to the side. It is a state to be contemplated with a bewildered mixture of wonder and horror.

On the other hand, in the literature of homosexuality—novels and stories by gay writers, or with gay heroes, or with love affairs between two men or two women at their center; choose your own terminology—there are amazingly few examples of the marriage narrative. The marriage, if it comes, comes at the end; or else the novel begins with a breakup. It is what literature prepares for or leads away from, not what literature contends with. Yet there are amazing stories to be told, of lesbians who buy houses together after forty-eight hours, or gay couples who invite extra lovers into their domestic lives, with banal or brutal results, or *ménages à trois* that last for decades. (Glenway Wescott lived in one.)

Why isn't anyone telling these stories? Why don't I tell these stories?

6.

AM I CRAZY, or have weddings never before been such big business? Half the shows on the Discovery Channel seem to me about planning weddings. (The other half tend to feature couples fixing up their houses or having babies.) Reality shows: Trista and Ryan's wedding. Movies: *My Big Fat Greek Wedding, The Wedding Planner, The Wedding Singer, Father of the Bride* (*1* and *2*), *Monsoon Wedding* (which ends with the heroine finding happiness in an arranged marriage, after her "true" love turns out to be a cad) . . . Bridal magazines: have you noticed that they're always the fattest? No shortage of ad pages there. Because everyone wants to choose the dress, the refreshments, the flower arrangements. There is the drama of the invitations. (One cousin of mine wrote a lengthy letter to my father, explaining why she had invited him and his wife to her wedding, but none of his children.)

There is the drama of the vows. (Should the children from a previous marriage be allowed in?) There is the drama of who sits at which table. The drama of whether or not the bride should change her name. The drama of where to register, which patterns to choose. And of course the bouquet. The damned bouquet.

Rarely is any event in ordinary life so heavily orchestrated, so overdetermined, as a wedding. It is the closest most of us get (who are not actors) to being on stage.

7.

A FRIEND OF mine—a lesbian—said to me once, "The thing is this. Isn't the whole point of being gay to rebel? To throw off the shackles of heterosexual oppression? To create new ways of living, instead of parroting the old ones?"

True. Yet with what horror do we regard the elderly queen who still devotes his life to the pursuit (usually in exchange for cash) of frequent and varied sex! "That's the wonderful thing about us," a particularly grotesque exemplar of the genre said to me a few years ago in Florence. "We never grow up."

Better—more dignified—to be part of a dapper, elderly couple. "Imagine! Two men together that long! What's your secret?"

To quote Mary Haines's mother in *The Women* (that gayest of marriage-defense movies), "It's being together at the end that counts."

8.

AND OF COURSE, what no one seems to remember these days is that long before gay marriage became the political hot potato that it is today, gay men and lesbians still had weddings. They didn't need no piece of paper from the city hall. They just did it.

I only ever went to one. This was in the mid-eighties. Rumor had it that the couple in question, a divinity student and a lawyer, decided to tie the knot because *Newsweek* had offered to put them on its cover—but only if their parents posed for the picture, too. And one set of parents refused. So the *Newsweek* cover was off, but the invitations had already gone out, and the wedding—the show—had to go on.

It was an almost painfully formal affair. A woman minister (Unitarian) performed the ceremony. A soprano sang one of those things that sopranos sing at weddings. Both grooms wore dark suits. Afterward, there was a reception in Brooklyn with canapés and a string quartet. The guests drank champagne and talked about where to get the best Australian wine. But there was no dancing.

Now I ask you: what's the point of a wedding reception if there's no dancing?

The marriage lasted three years.

9.

BACK IN THE old days, before gay couples had wedding announcements in the *New York Times,* people sometimes asked me if I and my boyfriend (my then boyfriend) ever thought about getting married. I replied caustically that in my view the only good reason to get married was for the presents, and as people were never going to give decent presents to two queers, what was the point? After all, most of the loot that my brother and sister pulled in at their weddings came not from my parents or their spouses' parents or even relatives, but from family friends, for whom this game of gift and take—I'll get something good for your kid if you promise to get something good for mine—had been going on since time immemorial. My brother and sister got china (two settings, one for everyday, one for company), silver *and* stainless, crystal *and* glass, towels, tablecloths, napkins, blenders, coffee grinders and coffee makers, and, of course, cash. Loads of cash. Indeed, because my sister's husband is Mexican-American, at her wedding, according to Mexican tradition, there was something called the "dollar dance," during which the guests danced with either the bride or the groom and afterward pinned a bill to her dress or his tuxedo. Like prostitution. By the time the dance was over, my sister and her husband were green as trees in spring. Needless to say, I only danced with my sister.

Do I sound bitter?

10.

IN GRACE PALEY'S story "Listening," a character named Cassie—a lesbian—confronts Faith, Paley's heroine and alter-ego, with a complaint. In "Faith's" stories, all their common friends make appearances. But not Cassie herself. "You've told everybody's story but mine," she tells Faith. "I don't even mean my whole story, that's my job. You probably can't. But I mean you've just omitted me from the other stories and I was there. In the restaurant and the train, right there. Where is Cassie? Where is *my* life? It's been women and men, women and men, fucking, fucking. Goddamnit, where the hell is my woman and woman, woman-loving life in all this?"

Women and men, women and men, fucking, fucking.

In February I saw Grace. I asked her if Cassie was real.

"No," Grace said. "She just came to me. I made her up."

It was as if Grace were doing a kind of penance, compensating for an act of exclusion of which no one had bothered to remind her—except herself. So she invented Cassie to offer the necessary rebuke.

II.

I'M NOT GOING to go the route of pretending that my relationship with Mark is any better than any heterosexual couple's. I'm not going to swan or claim superiority. Marriage is a mixed bag. Banal and blissful. Annoying. Companionable. An anchor. By which I mean, I'm glad to be inside one rather than gazing in at one, befuddled, from without.

The town where we live is, I suppose, liberal, by which I mean that here we don't have to pretend that our relationship is other than what it is. (Then again, we never have.) Everyone treats us as an ordinary married couple. Even my undergraduate students are blasé about it. Reared in a *Will and Grace* world, they *know* what gay is. So when a girl writes a story with a boy narrator, invariably some boy in the class says, "I think it's cool that the narrator is a lesbian."

The only problem is: what do I call Mark? When talking to my colleagues? To my students?

Boyfriend seems juvenile, after more than a dozen years. Lover is dated. Partner sounds like a law firm. Companion makes me think of obituaries. I suppose I could go the way of the Italians and call him my colleague or associate. Or I could use the term in fashion in Forster's day, and call him my friend. Or my comrade. Somehow I can't imagine calling him my husband. I'm sorry, but it just sounds silly to me.

In the end, to save trouble, I usually just call him Mark.

12.

THIS YEAR THE university has a new president. He is, as we say, "gay friendly." They say that soon—maybe even in the fall—he'll announce a domestic partnership plan, in order to bring the university in line with the ones of the stature to which it aspires. The next question is: what will we have to do to show that we're domestic partners? The question after that: if gay marriage comes, will we do it? We emphatically support every gay couple's right to marry—but do we want to marry ourselves?

I'll just say this: certainly not for the presents. We've already got the dishes, the stainless, the tablecloths. We've got the blender and the coffee grinder. (But not the china. Not the silver.) No one gave these things to us. We bought them ourselves.

Vows

BY FRANCINE PROSE

JUNE 15, 1897. OSCAR FINGAL O'Flahertie Wills Wilde and Lord Alfred Douglas were married yesterday in the First Unitarian Church in Toronto, Canada. Mr. Wilde, 43, is a writer, author of such successful plays as *The Importance of Being Earnest,* and of the controversial and critically acclaimed best seller, *The Picture of Dorian Gray.* He studied at Oxford, where he received a B.A. He is the son of Lady Jane Francesca "Speranza" Wilde, an author and translator, and the late Sir William Wilde, a Dublin ear surgeon. Mr. Wilde's previous marriage, to the former Constance Lloyd, ended in divorce.

Lord Douglas, 27, known to his friends as "Bosie," was also educated at Oxford. He is the son of the Marquess of Queensberry, an amateur poet, serious boxer, and hunter, and the Marchioness, Lady Queensberry, of Bracknell. Lord Douglas is also a poet, best known for having written the line, "the love that dare not speak its name."

The Salome-themed reception, inspired by one of Mr. Wilde's plays, was held at Chor Bazaar, a popular Toronto night spot. The friends and well-wishers who attended the ceremony agreed that, for Oscar and Bosie, the path that led to the altar had been an unusually thorny one. They were introduced six years before, by a mutual friend who brought Lord Douglas to Mr. Wilde's Tite Street home. It was obvious that sparks flew between them when Mr. Wilde gave Lord Douglas a deluxe copy of his novel and offered to help him with his studies at Oxford.

Still, romance took a while to blossom.

"Oscar was also so preoccupied," recalled Lord Douglas. "He was always writing something. Plays, essays . . ." Not long after they met, a professional trip to France separated the pair. "Oscar was such a sensation in Paris, and met so many famous French writers, I felt sure that he had forgotten me." But fate reunited them in London.

The newlyweds told slightly different stories about how the courtship evolved. "Oscar was all over me," said Lord Douglas. "Letters, poems, gifts." Mr. Wilde remembered it somewhat differently. "Bosie came to me for help over the matter of a rather . . . reckless letter. He was being blackmailed. My lawyer took care of everything." In any case, it soon became clear that this was the real thing.

Inevitably, there were problems. "Bosie was a handful," remembered Mr. Wilde, referring to Mr. Douglas's notoriously quick temper and money-management problems. And the couple's families were slow to get on board. The Marquess's opposition to the match was well known, and Constance Wilde was less than thrilled by this new development in her husband's life. "I never took his previous flings seriously," said the former Mrs. Wilde, who attended the ceremony, along with her two children. "This time I knew it was different. But still it took me awhile to see that Oscar and Bosie were made for each other."

For quite some time, Mr. Wilde and Lord Douglas were inseparable.

"Long engagements give people the opportunity of finding out each other's character before marriage, which is never advisable," Mr. Wilde observed.

"Frankly," said André Gide, a fellow writer and friend of Mr. Wilde's, also in attendance at the wedding, "there were plenty of times when all of us doubted that Bosie and Oscar would make it. They're both pretty complicated guys, and *mon dieu*, the trials didn't make it any easier for them."

"All trials," Mr. Wilde put in, "are trials for one's life."

He was, of course, referring to the disastrous legal proceedings that began when Mr. Wilde decided to sue his partner's father for libel. After losing his case, Mr. Wilde was charged with Gross Indecency. He was convicted, and sentenced to two years in prison. During his incarceration, most people assumed that the couple had split up for good.

"Gosh," said Bosie. "Oscar wrote a whole book about me, about our relationship being over, full of all kinds of accusations . . ."

Mr. Wilde smiled. "The fact was, Bosie waited for me till I got out of jail."

Lord Douglas said that Mr. Wilde began to write him every day. Eventually, they arranged to meet in France.

"He was weeping at the railroad station," Lord Douglas recalled. "So I kind of knew right then."

But it wasn't until a trip to Naples that Mr. Wilde proposed.

Mr. Wilde gazed at the billowing drapery that gave the nightclub the look of a sultan's palace. Then Mr. Wilde, who is famous among his friends for his witty aphorisms, added, "Marriage is the triumph of imagination over intelligence." Lord Douglas gave him a strange look, and then the happy couple laughed.

NOT ONLY DID IT never happen, but it never would have happened, not even if it could have. Let's say the laws were the opposite of what they actually were; let's say that instead of jailing Oscar Wilde and punishing him horribly for the crime of loving another human being, the state had allowed, indeed encouraged, him and Lord Alfred Douglas to marry, to celebrate and affirm their love, while at the same time obtaining the privileges that the state reserves for married couples.

Wilde had already been married. His wedding, to Constance Lloyd, was nothing like the one I have imagined above. By the time Constance accepted him, Wilde had already proposed unsuccessfully to two other women. A distant relative of the Wilde family's Dublin friends, Constance was twenty-three, intelligent, well educated, and a bit arty. Her father was dead, her estranged mother remarried. She lived with her wealthy grandfather.

Wilde must have felt some pressure to get married, but he also appears to have had a genuine affection for Constance and to have wanted children. Besides which, her grandfather had money. So Wilde got married for all the reasons people marry, unless it happens to be for love.

Oscar and Constance were married in 1884, at St. James' Church, quietly, because her grandfather was ill. Wilde served as his own wedding planner, designing the gowns for his bride and her attendants. His creation for Constance was a gown (satin, pearls, gauze, white blossoms) fit for a princess in a Pre-Raphaelite painting.

In 1893, Wilde left her and went to stay with Douglas. Constance considered divorce, but gave up the idea, to which her husband was opposed. Husband and wife became estranged, reconciled, estranged again, and eventually stopped seeing one another. But they were still married when Constance died, after an operation on her spine, in 1898.

One assumes that married life provided Constance with so much to endure and rise above that her feelings were barely singed by the fact that her husband seemed unable to resist making jokes about the institution of marriage. And Wilde must have discovered that marriage jokes could be depended on to get a laugh from the theater audience. Some of his aphorisms are snappy and facile: "I have always been of the opinion that a man about to get married should know either everything or nothing." "Marriage is the one subject on which all women agree and all men disagree." Others are simply arch: "The proper basis for marriage is a mutual misunderstanding." But still more have an undercurrent of genuine contempt and even cruelty running just beneath their witty surface: "Twenty years of romance make a woman look like a ruin; twenty years of marriage make her look like a public building." "Men marry because they are tired, women because they are curious; both are disappointed." And finally: "A man can be happy with any woman, so long as he does not love her."

Wilde was joking, obviously. Still, it's hard to imagine such statements being uttered, even in jest, by the starry-eyed, hopeful, idealistic couples—gay and straight—who populate the marriage announcement pages of our local newspapers, and who provide the copy for the sort of article on which I've based my account of the Wilde-Douglas nuptials.

At the present moment, there is a sort of low-energy debate transpiring on various Web sites and blogs concerning the question of whether or not Oscar Wilde would have supported gay marriage. This debate has apparently been fueled by the appearance of a new book, *The Unmasking of Oscar Wilde*, by a Catholic biographer named Joseph Pearce, who claims that Wilde was a lifelong would-be Catholic, who asked to be received into the Church on his deathbed. According to Pearce, Wilde considered homosexuality a pathology, and would have opposed gay marriage. But as the on-line author of the "Pansexual Sodomite" column writes: "Speculating on how a man of another time would respond to contemporary events is one of those bad habits that merit a spanking. . . . Though it might merit a birch rod I have as much right to say what Wilde would feel about gay marriage. So I'll opine that he would have been first in line for a marriage license (hopefully for Robbie Ross not Bosie)."

Both Pearce and his critic miss the point, which is that Wilde's feelings about marriage had, I would argue, less to do with religion or sexual politics than about his deep distrust and healthy scorn for institutions in general, and bourgeois Victorian institutions in particular. In his wonderfully peculiar essay, "The Soul of Man Under Socialism," Wilde tries to persuade us that "When Jesus talks about the poor he simply means personalities, just as when he talks about the rich he simply means people who have not developed their personalities. . . . He said to man, 'You have a wonderful personality. Develop it. Be yourself.'" Wilde predicts and welcomes the disappearance of marriage in its present form: "Individualism accepts this and makes it fine. It converts the abolition of legal restraint into a form of freedom that will help the full development of personality, and make the love of man and woman more wonderful, more beautiful, and more ennobling. Jesus knew this. He rejected the claims of family life . . ."

Together with Bosie, Wilde embraced not only homosexual love and culture but the underside of gay life. Monogamy or sexual fidelity seem never to have been considered a necessary condition of their relationship, and both men consorted with young prostitutes, or "renters" as they were called. Wilde liked the idea of himself as a rebel, an outrageous outsider, even a criminal, of a certain dandified sort. According to his biographer Richard Ellmann, "The excitement of doing something considered wrong, and the professional avarice of the blackmailing, extortionate, faithless boys, may have been as important for Wilde as sexual gratification." Unlike the gay or straight engaged couples who sign up with the bridal registry of their local department stores, Oscar Wilde seems to have had little desire to be embraced and accepted by middle-class society. He simply did not want to be persecuted by it, which of course he was.

Though I myself have been happily married (knock on wood) for almost thirty years, I—like Oscar Wilde, I would like to believe—could hardly have less faith in the institution or less interest in having the state or the church regulate my private life. My husband and I would have been less likely to have gotten married (which we did in a civil ceremony, an absolutely minimalist affair at the home of the justice of the peace, a ceremony during which the justice's children were required to turn down the volume on their TV set, but not to turn it off) if the state had guaranteed that our rights (regarding medical decisions, health insurance, inheritance, and so forth) would be exactly the same as if we were cohabitating, or joined in a civil union. It's not that I don't believe in ritual and ceremony, but rather that I think the affirmation and commitment symbolized by such rituals should be integrated and expressed in every second of every day, every moment of one's ordinary life.

Make no mistake. I believe that gay and straight people should be able to get married if they wish. Just as they should be able to live together without what is commonly known as the benefit of clergy. People should be free to live alone, as couples, in conventional and unconventional, extended and nuclear, families—to make their own decisions about all this, to find any way that helps them get through this problematic, difficult, rewarding, joyous, and frequently painful process known as human life.

But what scares me about marriage—gay and straight— is much the same thing that, I can't help imagining, disturbed Oscar Wilde. At its worst, marriage does what the imaginary marriage announcement that I've invented for the Wilde-Douglas union does; that is, it traffics in banalities and clichés, emphasizes the laws of succession, maintains the status quo, reinforces the stratifications of social positions, subverts the individual, and turns what is private into something public. It encourages us to think about our romantic, sexual, and family life in ways that are unrealistic and ultimately harmful; it sets up impossible expectations that most of us can hardly hope or attempt to fulfill. Finally, and most importantly, it is an institution, and like so many institutions, it attempts to persuade its members that it is necessary and right, that its way is the only way, and that everyone should belong, and follow its rules.

When we consider the progress we have made from Wilde's time, when "gross indecency" was a crime punishable by imprisonment, to our own era, when the last state laws attempting to regulate sex between consenting adults are being overturned, one by one, it seems probable that—regardless of the Christian Right's pressure on our government to pass a constitutional amendment banning same-sex marriage—it will eventually be possible for pairs of gay men and women to join the other couples waiting in line, in every city and state, at the marriage license bureau. In the worst-case scenario—the sort of eventuality that, one senses, Wilde feared—the institution of marriage will reveal its most restrictive and conservative face. Weddings will steadily grow more ostentatious, pairings will reflect and confirm the gradations of status and class, and unwed gay couples will be made to feel the same pressures and disapproval to which unmarried, cohabiting heterosexual lovers were subjected in earlier eras. But I'd rather hope for the best. I'd like to think that the gay community will bring its creativity—the spirit and inventiveness that have transformed the worlds of theater, design, and art—to marriage, and make of it something brighter, looser, more capacious and complex than the predictable, orderly Noah's Ark procession that Oscar Wilde regarded with such disdain, and such fear.

The Good Marriage;
or, The Kiss of the Fat Man

BY STACEY D'ERASMO

THERE IS A MOVIE that I love very much called *L'Atalante*, by Jean Vigo. Made in 1934, it is the story of a woman from a small French village who marries the owner of a barge. The movie begins with the wedding of these two: the bride's long white veil flutters behind her, over the dirt and grass on the hills, as she makes her way with her new husband from the church to the barge where they will live together. On the barge as well are an old sailor named le père Jules, and a young boy. They embark, or perhaps it would be more accurate to say that she embarks, because the men are making a journey they have made many times before. For her, it is new, and as it turns out, transformative; she enters the world of experience, first, literally, as the barge moves toward Paris, but second, and more importantly, she uncovers an abundant internal world of yearning, curiosity, and imagination both with, and in opposition to, her husband.

The movie glows and broods simultaneously in lush black and white. The soundscape is spare and lonely, pockmarked by the wind, the knocks of the boat. It was Vigo's last film; he died young of tuberculosis just after completing it. The film wasn't particularly admired when it was first released, but when it was reissued in 1990, it was recognized as a masterpiece. That's when I saw it, and I've seen it several times since. The film is lauded for many reasons, but it has always been highly resonant to me as an image of marriage, a houseboat that is itself a dense, ambiguous world moving through a larger world of great density and ambiguity. The lovers on *L'Atalante* argue and reconcile, make love, both wound and liberate one another. One of the pivotal scenes in the movie occurs when the bride ventures into the quarters of le père Jules. He takes off his shirt and shows her his myriad tattoos; then, even more astonishing to her, he shows her some of the exotic talismans and treasure he's picked up during his many years at sea: a particularly lethal Spanish knife, a photo of a naked native girl, a pair of severed hands, an elephant tusk, a fan. The bride is fascinated by this world-liness, though her reverie is interrupted by her new hus-band, who storms into the room and, fearing that she's been up to no good with le père Jules, begins throwing things around. She is curious, awake, impressionable; he is in love, jealous, afraid to lose her. Around this tension the marriage, and the movie, revolves. It all ends happily, more or less; the bride runs away to explore the wonders of Paris but then re-turns, and their boat sails on.

In the ambivalent persona of the curious bride, the com-plicatedly happy ending, the movie poses a question, and a hope, that I find very compelling: what is a good marriage? On both the left and the right these days, that is not the question. The political question of the moment has to do with privilege, who gets what benefits and under what name and when. The continual invocation of licenses suggests permission, access: to health care, tax breaks, parental rights, cultural recognition. It seems to be assumed in a nonspecific sort of way that we all know what we mean by "marriage" and that, of course, we are all referring to a last-ing intimate structure in which people are kind and loving to one another, emotionally faithful if not always strictly monogamous, and reliable. As in any emergency, there doesn't seem to be time to reflect on what a good marriage might actually be, or, indeed, what marriage is. Philosophical questions are a luxury, if not a scandal, during a war.

And yet. Whether or not my government grants me the right during my lifetime to be legally married to another woman, the constant contemporary drumbeat of the word "marriage" reminds me, like a recurring dream, of something I have much desired and have avidly pursued through several long relationships, something that the government can't actually bestow or withhold: the good marriage.

But what is that?

A few years before my grandmother died, she was—not for the first time—so deeply infuriated with my grandfather that she hurled a knife at him. Fortunately for him, she missed. They had been married for more than sixty years, raised three children together, sometimes fought bitterly, and were inseparable to the end. During the long time that my grandmother was dying, my grandfather said that he had just remembered that they must have played together as small children in the Italian ghettos of Newark, where they both grew up. He based this memory on how close their respective houses had been; he was sure that it was true. What struck me was the fact that, as she was going away from him, he was reaching back to fuse them together from the beginning. He was getting more time with her retrospectively. He has always been an aggressive, talkative, very solid man, built like a stevedore; he has a strong, briny Newark accent to this day. He has never seemed less than formidable, but to my surprise he didn't hide any of his sorrow or hope from the rest of us. His need for her was raw. Almost to the moment of her death he was adamant that she would get well and on the day of her funeral he refused to join the rest of the family for dinner that evening at a local restaurant. "I was married to her for a long time," he said. "I have a lot to think about."

I wondered if he was thinking about that knife as he sat alone in their house, and whether she'd meant to miss, or not. For my grandparents, the question of the good marriage was, I think, somewhat overshadowed by the fact that theirs was a Catholic marriage; will, not choice, was explicitly written into the bargain. Something much larger than themselves would keep them together whether they liked it or not, forever; death, in this context, almost seemed like a breach of contract. But that mandate didn't mean that they were indifferent to one another. On the contrary. During her illness, I was astonished, and a little embarrassed, to get a glimpse into the incredible force of their bond, undone as they were by extremity. It was more intimate than anything explicitly sexual, and it made that knife not so simple. Would it have been a better marriage if no knives were thrown? Undoubtedly. But would it have been a better marriage, or even a good one, if the drive that propelled the knife were absent? I don't know. How many knives are too many?

Two generations removed from that kind of marriage, I want something even more impossible. Wound into my DNA is a belief in the union of the unlike, that the good marriage is the marriage of difference in ways that go far beyond, or beneath, gender difference. If it were my job to populate the ark, I'd put the giraffe with the emu, the swan with the monkey, the fox with the turtle. There's no great mystery as to why this should be the case: my parents were very different from one another ethnically, temperamentally, religiously, and in many other ways. In their difference, they signified not the smooth continuation of some universal, homogeneous species, but the rough invention of the new world. Eventually, they divorced, but the residue of their dream is the substrate of mine.

For better or worse, then, it is my fate that I find the most spark, the most romance and adventure, in marriages with palpable edges of dissimilarity; that is, marriages in which one can feel, quite distinctly, the continually shifting place where two people meet, disband, and meet again; marriages in which, to return to *L'Atalante,* Paris is not only always an option, but in which the marriage itself is Paris: a city, a radical set of juxtapositions, a continually incommensurate union. Having been born at the intersection of two very different people, I still long to reunite the dissimilar, to build in my own house the capacious capital where they might meet.

To want a marriage like a city: is that excessive? Probably, it is. Probably, it's ridiculous. When asked, the gay men and women lining up for marriage licenses say that they want the myriad concrete benefits that accrue to married straight people. Daily reality is laundry, dog pee, groceries, in-laws. There is a strong strain in pop and not-so-pop psychology at the moment that shies away from the lyrical when it comes to marriage, that trusts steadiness and looks askance at rapture. Good love is valued over infatuation, daily bread over opium. "Soul mate," in this practical vocabulary, is synonymous with "mutual craziness." Instead, the language of partnership is invoked, two people in a kayak soberly paddling downstream, wearing life jackets.

Perhaps that is the good marriage, but it's not a marriage I've ever had, and I don't mean because same-sex marriage licenses weren't available. The juice in marriage, for me, as for the curious bride in *L'Atalante,* is epistemological: it's a way of knowing—self, other, world—that can only be known through union with, and sometimes in opposition to, another person. Moreover, it is something that, as in writing novels, you can only know if you have thrown your entire hand onto the table, if the stakes are very high. There is much, of course, that we can know by ourselves, much that we know through family and friends and the passing day, but the kind of knowing that comes through enduring desire, through sexual union, through, even, profound disappointment and searing lack, has always seemed unique and absolutely vital to me. Like the curious bride, I want to go somewhere I haven't been before; I want to know something I could not have known otherwise. This is probably even more of an old-fashioned belief than that in longevity or monogamy—the belief in the irreducible thereness of someone else, their essential, lasting foreignness. The belief, in other words, that marriage is not a noun, like a piece of furniture, but a verb, "to marry": a continual reaching.

The monadic, self-enclosed, modern vocabulary of marriage tends to slight this dimension, as if there is really nothing that you can experience with another person that you couldn't replicate perfectly well alone, and in the good marriage, apparently, both people are secure in this knowledge. Everyone is a "complete person," like a little corporation. "A mate," says Oprah, "is only there to give you back to yourself." Really? Then what? Just as we seem, as a culture, to be highly resistant to the reality and irrevocability of loss, we are deeply suspicious of the possibility that other people bring things into our lives that only they can bring and that can't be replicated at will. We like to think that we can make, and remake, the world by ourselves, endlessly: this is thought to be independence. But there is a cosmopolis that any marriage, even a bad marriage, makes that literally wouldn't exist if it were left to either person alone. The houseboat, the Seine, and Paris are, in a sense, a landscape that the newlyweds' presence not only explores, but invents. If the marriage disintegrates, it's like Atlantis: a lost city. It's not so hard, considering this, to have sympathy with the destructive jealousy of the husband. He knows what's at stake. Just as Berlin is not Johannesburg, every mutually invented geography has a singular, ineffable quality that is much more than the sum of its bricks and boulevards.

To my mind, the good marriage is not one in which both people are securely self-enclosed, mutually reflective spheres, but the opposite. The good marriage is one in which both people in it can bear the vulnerability of the knowledge that neither of them is capable of sole possession of the realm—a realm that only comes into existence in the space between them. The myriad stories of people—straight people, gay people, all people—splitting up and grabbing kids, houses, pets, friends seem like variations on the myth of Narcissus, suffused with a fatal fantasy of oneself as the entire world. Anyone who has ever ended a longstanding relationship knows how futile these grabs are, how quickly the totemic magic drains away from objects and once beloved places. After a break-up many years ago, I let several boxes of things I thought it very important to claim sit in a damp basement until the boxes began to rot. When I finally unpacked the boxes, most of what was in there seemed flat, cheap. The things were just things, the animus gone.

"I was married to her for a long time," my grandfather said. "I have a lot to think about." He's given away closets-full of her clothes; he goes into the garage for long periods of time to rummage through various trunks and boxes. He's very busy. On his upper right arm is a tattoo of a heart with an arrow through it and her name that he had inscribed just before he married her, in 1937. The blue is so faded it's nearly part of his skin. A friend of mine, a young man, has a vivid tattoo of flames on the underside of one forearm and a tattoo of a hula girl on the underside of another. "I had these done when I met M," he told me, speaking of the man who changed his life and for whom he moved across a continent. When le père Jules shows the bride his marked body, he's not only showing her where he's been, but, obliquely, who he's loved. The good marriage, to me, is less license than it is tattoo, the conscious acknowledgment that we mark one another, change one another; those marks simultaneously become a part of us and serve as a continual reminder of foreignness, otherness, choice, loss. It would be a very different spectacle if, instead of lining up outside city halls for marriage licenses, gay people were lining up to tattoo one another, and yet I think it would be more accurate. Indeed, it would be more accurate to say that most of us are already tattooed, crosshatched with the imprint of the people we have loved deeply.

It is customary in journalistic boilerplate to refer to same-sex marriage as "a divisive issue," meaning that some people think it should be allowed and others don't. But same-sex marriage is also internally divisive, both within the gay community and within individual people, because it forces the question of whether or not one believes in the possibility of marriage at all, much less a good one. As heterosexuals on reality TV shows auction one another off as spouses, it can fairly be said that gay people might be the last citizens of the planet to evince such sincere faith in marrying. Do you believe? is the sub-rosa question of the hour, a question that's much more complicated than the clear-cut issue of civil rights. That answer, at the end of the day, is probably as personal, and as varied, as sexual preference. Some brides never leave their villages; some run away to Paris and don't come back; some return to the houseboat, which will continue with its full cargo of fantasy and reality, love and anger, its odd-lot jumble of passengers, to other ports of call.

What sort of bride you really are—in fairy tales, and in the movies, this is revealed by a test of fate. Recently, my lover and I were in Sicily in a medieval town called Erice. In Erice are the ruins of the Temple of Venus. You have to walk or drive up a long hill to get to the temple, and when you finally get there you see an assemblage of stone half-walls, weed-strewn places that used to be courtyards, shattered doorways, an ancient, dry well that was once sacred. In the dark, cold heap of rocks that constitutes the entrance to the Temple of Venus stands a voluble, elderly, fat man. You give him your money, which he puts in his pocket, and then, before you can go into the temple itself, he has to tell you a long story in Italian that my lover and I pretended we understood. We nodded. I caught a few narrative threads: temple prostitutes, mysterious sacrifices, holy orgies, some wars, etc.

Even with my nominal Italian I could tell that the fat man's sense of history was shaky at best. He clearly loves to tell this story, at length, but at the end of it comes the real point of his tale. Can he kiss you? It seemed obvious to me that you couldn't really enter the Temple of Venus, even if you were walking through it, without the kiss of the fat man, who has told his story, and kissed the ladies, thousands of times before. It's shtick, and nevertheless you either buy it or you don't as you wait your turn to get into the ruins. Among many other things, the question of same-sex marriage is a referendum on the fat man. It means nothing about the law, or about what anyone else should do, to say that I offered my cheek.

Crock-Pots: A Confession

BY KATHLEEN FINNERAN

WHEN I WAS A SOPHOMORE in high school, I bought my English teacher a Crock-Pot for her birthday. "Who's that for?" my older sister pressed when she came home from work earlier than I expected and walked in on me wrapping the box. I cleared a place on the floor of our bedroom closet and attempted to conceal the wrapped package under what I hoped would look like a naturally occurring clump of shoes and clothes, rather than a pile purposely arranged. It's hard to hide a Crock-Pot, especially in a closet that was, if not compulsively maintained by my mother (as was the rest of our house), at least regularly consulted to satisfy her sense of order.

"Who is that *for?*" my sister kept asking. She had been let off early that night from her job at the mall, where she worked as a sales clerk at Cards 'n Such. Business was slow because of the snow. I had trekked through it myself to buy the Crock-Pot, not walking all the way to the mall, but to the Walgreens that had just opened a straight shot up the highway. I'd cut a coupon from a circular advertising the store's grand-opening specials. CROCK-POTS $23.99.

The last week of February, it was dark out after dinner. My mother worked nights, and I told my father I was going to my friend's house on the next street to study. Hills of old snow hugged each side of the highway and it was difficult at times to judge the depth and firmness of the drifts. One moment, I would be standing on top of a hard mountain of snow, secure, invincible, exhilarated by the cold, the close rush of cars, and my mission to buy a Crock-Pot for a teacher I adored. The next, I would be buried to my hips, surprised by a sink hole on the far side of the same hill that, seconds earlier, had supported my full weight, my secrets, all my adolescent awkwardness and wonder, all my anxiety and awe.

At Walgreens, I was faced with a decision that I had not known I would have to make: avocado, almond, or burnt orange. The coupon had given no clue. The Crock-Pot came in a choice of three colors. I narrowed it down to the avocado or almond. (Why was the orange burnt? I wondered.)

I had never been inside my teacher's house, did not know her taste in décor or the colors in her kitchen. I had seen the outside of her house many times—a redbrick bungalow with gray shutters and hedges that no one ever trimmed. I drove past it whenever my father took me out driving on my permit. If he noticed that we always ended up going down the same street, a few miles from where we lived, he never said. I suspect he did notice, but did not ask. He had always been hesitant to discover more than he wanted or needed to know about us, preferring instead that information about his five children come to him in controlled dispatches, spread out over time, usually presented to him in some palatable manner by my mother. Once informed, he would report the content of these briefings back to us. "Your mother tells me," he would say. "Your mother tells me you haven't found new friends here . . . Your mother tells me that things at school aren't as easy for you as they might seem . . . Your mother tells me," when I was ten, and twelve, and seventeen, and twenty. "Your mother tells me," he calls today to say, and I am forty-six.

"Kathleen?" he called out from the family room when he heard me come home on the night I bought the Crock-Pot. I stood in the darkened kitchen, just inside the back door, and listened for the whereabouts of everyone else. Where were my little sister, Kelly, my younger brother, Sean?

"Kathleen?" my father called again.

"Yes," I answered, standing as quietly as I could in the dark, careful not to allow any hint that I had carried a package into the house. I strained to hear the slightest movement, any indication that he might be getting up and coming toward the kitchen. A red dial glowed from the front of the dishwasher, the only light in the room, and as I stood there, listening, considering the best route to take to my bedroom, the machine hissed into its final cycle with a sigh, an exhalation so familiar and enveloping it felt almost visceral, a kind of warm, vaporous comfort that I imagined might magically transform itself from sound into substance if need be, readily concealing this purchase that I would be hard-pressed to explain to my father.

At that period in my life, I was just starting to sense that there was something different about me, but I had no real idea what it was. I didn't know anything about homosexuality until I was out of high school. I didn't even know that homosexuals existed. I knew that wearing green and yellow on a certain day of the week—was it Wednesday? Thursday?—meant that you were queer, but I didn't realize that the word carried any sexual connotations. I simply thought it meant that you were strange. It seems incredible that a teenager growing up in the 1970s could be so unaware of the world, but I was. Most of my time was spent with my family—in a world that was solely heterosexual, it seemed.

I hadn't yet felt any sexual desire for anyone, not even for the teacher on whom I had a crush. I simply craved her attention. I longed for her to recognize me, to see me as more than just a student in her English class, but I didn't understand that she was the start of something. No, what I thought was different about me back then, what I thought was beginning to make me seem odd, to cause the few friends I had to become fewer, were these strange whirls of imagination that would take over my mind, almost seizure-like in their strength, but in the end not even very interesting: a dishwasher whose familiar hiss could somehow shroud you, inanimate objects that would always come to your aid, spewing a cloud of smoke here, causing a distraction there, not nearly as spectacular as the alternate worlds that some dreamers create. Nonetheless, my mind thrilled me. Its meanderings lifted me. Its meanderings *were* me. The risks I took in my teenage years were not ones of inquiring whether any of my friends had feelings for girls rather than boys. The risks I took back then, before finally silencing myself against ridicule, were of a much more intimate nature, the forays of someone still unaware of her own innocence, someone whose exuberance had not yet been eroded by the hard-edged encounters of adolescence. "Can you imagine what would happen if . . . ," I would venture. "I was just thinking what it would be like if . . ." And my friends would stare at me blankly, at best, or, as was more often the case, mock my idea simply by repeating it back to me with a cultivated attitude of coolness and derision.

"If only the walls could talk," my mother once said when

she walked in on my brother and me conspiring something in the kitchen. "If only the stove could sing," Sean shot back, laughing. Comrade, I called him.

"What are you doing in there?" my father yelled from the family room.

"Nothing," I said. The couch squeaked and I imagined him coming into the kitchen, catching me with the Crock-Pot. A long moment passed.

"Sean and Kelly need to get their hair washed after they're finished watching this show," he finally called out. "Can you help them with that?"

"Sure," I said, and I slipped upstairs with the Crock-Pot, avoiding the family room where I figured all three of them must have been watching TV.

I had gone with the green. It seemed the safest choice. Not as loud as the burnt orange. Not as dull as the almond. "Oh! How perfect! All of my appliances are avocado!" I imagined her saying when she opened it.

• • •

"I can't accept this," is what she said instead. She looked around to see if anyone else in the faculty lounge noticed that I had surprised her with a Crock-Pot. "My birthday," she said to some teachers at the next table.

"I heard you say that you wanted one," I said. I had overheard her telling another teacher that she wished she'd had a Crock-Pot so she could dump all the ingredients of a meal into it in the morning and have dinner all ready to eat when she got home. "Your evenings will be freed up," I said, repeating what I had heard her say to her colleague.

"Oh," she said, as if she were trying to recall the conversation.

Her birthday had been no secret. She had hung a calendar in her room at the start of the semester with a banner above it that read COUNTING DOWN THE DAYS 'TIL MISS T. TURNS 30! She had joked about it, telling us that if we had anything we wanted to confide in her, we had better do it before the big day. She was one of a handful of teachers at the school who were young and considered cool. After her birthday she'd be over the hill, she warned, and would have no clue how to communicate with us teenagers. We'd better make the most of her while we could.

I had tried a few times to confide in her, but I had managed only to tell her how much I liked her class. In truth, I liked *her* more than I liked her class, a sophomore honors seminar on the Romantic poets. "You'll go far!" she wrote on one of my papers. "You've got what it takes!" she put on another. She laid her hand on my back once and left it there while she stood behind me reading Byron's "She Walks in Beauty" to the class. Oh, how I wished it had been one of his longer works.

Sensing my disappointment, she kept the Crock-Pot. I must have looked crestfallen when she had begun to refuse it. In fact, I probably felt panicked: How would I sneak it into the house again? I couldn't walk all the way back to Walgreens without going home first. Would Walgreens even let me return it? What had I done with the receipt? I could handle the hills of snow again if I had to. My real worry was that my mother might discover the Crock-Pot before I could return it. She would confront me by simply leaving it out in the open, on the kitchen table, or the lower landing of the steps. It would sit there, no mention of it being made, until I could no longer stand the silence, and without even asking a single question, she would get me to confess to her

why I had a Crock-Pot in my closet. (She would have already asked my older sister, who would feign ignorance, not
so much out of allegiance to me, but in keeping with her
current life's credo: the less that involved her, the better.
Though there would be some aspect of loyalty as well.
"Who's that for?" she had asked after she walked in on me
wrapping the box. "Oh, yeah? She's cool," she had said when
I told her I planned to give the Crock-Pot to Miss T. the next
day for her birthday.)

If my teacher had not, in the end, accepted the Crock-Pot,
it would have taken me months to repair the damage it
would have done me with my parents, should my mother
have found it. "Your mother tells me you spent $23.99 on a
Crock-Pot for your teacher," my father would say. That would
be the part that would take them the longest to reconcile:
That I would have spent that much money on someone. The
fact that I was buying a gift that was, to say the least, a bit
out of the ordinary, for a female teacher on whom I had a
crush, would have, I'm sure, been a lesser issue. My father
had been unemployed for months. My mother worked nights
and weekends. It was the $23.99 that would have worried

them, the disregard for money that it represented, not that there might be something slightly odd about their daughter.

My teacher thanked me and took the Crock-Pot home. In the faculty lounge, after she had opened the gift, it had taken me only a few seconds to realize that I had done something wrong. Her discomfort in front of the other teachers was palpable, and the few moments that it took for her to first reject, and then accept, the present (so conspicuous in both its size and wrapping) passed awkwardly between us. Later that afternoon, in our seminar on the Romantic poets, a few other kids in the class gave her gifts as well, but none could be compared, in any way, to the Crock-Pot. One gift, I remember, was a T-shirt that had some catchy phrase printed on the back about growing older. I don't remember the phrase, but I remember thinking, as she held it up, that it would be too small.

To my surprise, the next week she invited me to her house for dinner. She would make a meal in the Crock-Pot, she said. When I arrived, her boyfriend answered the door and introduced himself. He seemed sincere when he said how much they enjoyed having the Crock-Pot. She gave him a look. "What?" he said. She pointed out that his comment made it obvious that the two of them were living together (it hadn't made it obvious to me) and that that was something she didn't want known around school. The school district would frown upon it, she said. After we finished eating, she went to the back of the house to get some books she wanted to give me, books she said that I might not come across on my own. As I waited in the kitchen for her, I realized that the burnt orange would have been better.

I WAS THINKING about all of this today—some thirty years later—because a friend of mine called to tell me the outcome of a political fracas here in Missouri over when our state's proposed constitutional amendment banning same-sex marriage would be put on the ballot. Missouri's Democratic leadership pushed to get the issue on the ballot for the August primaries, while the Republicans hoped to block that effort and have the issue decided upon in November's general elections. The Democrats feared that placement of the issue on the November ballot might aid a Bush reelection by bringing greater numbers of conservative voters to the polls. The Republicans feared that an August vote would be detrimental to the passage of the amendment because significantly fewer numbers of Missouri's voters go to the polls in the primaries. Also, putting the issue on the August ballot would drastically reduce the time available to proselytize about this important opportunity, one that would allow voters both to legitimize their hatred for homosexuals and squash the civil rights of their fellow Americans in one painless pull of the lever (or, in Missouri's case, one easy push of the stylus into the appropriate hole).

My friend who phoned was jubilant. "We got August!" she said and referred me to an article in the *St. Louis Post-Dispatch*.

"Oh happy day," I told her as I skimmed the article.

"You don't understand," she said. "This is good for us. There's a much greater chance it won't pass now."

This particular optimistic friend of mine has been "not married" for seventeen years. She and her partner met working for a Christian ministry group in Guatemala, helping to build houses. They are schoolteachers and devote much of their free time in service to others. In addition, they are evil and the institution of marriage should be safeguarded against them.

Later this month two of my dearest friends, Georgia and Alice, will celebrate the anniversary of their Holy Union. Standing before family and friends—in the house where I happen now to live—they made their commitment to each other in a ceremony presided over by a minister of the Metropolitan Community Church. They will have been "not married" for twenty-nine years.

Sometimes, when I am sitting in my house, in the room where they did not get married, I wonder what that day must have been like for them. They had taken the long road around to each other. In her twenties, Georgia had made an earnest attempt at marriage to a man. It did not work out, but she was blessed with two children, who have, in turn, blessed her with five grandchildren. Hers is a family of many ethnicities and faiths. She sings the chorus of "We Are the World" jokingly as she shows me the latest batch of pictures of her kids and grandkids, her African-American granddaughter dancing, her Vietnamese twin grandsons testing out their new boots in a puddle. As an associate dean in the art school of a local university, she has been the advisor, confidante, and all-around guardian to generations of young artists. A scholarship fund in her name was recently bestowed upon the university by a grateful parent.

Until her early forties, Alice was a missionary doctor in Pakistan, where she worked to improve health care for women. After coming home to the United States, she turned her attentions to psychiatry and devoted much of her practice to helping people come to terms with issues of sexual identity. She is an active and respected member of her Episcopalian church.

When I sit in my house, in the room where Georgia and Alice were not married, I sometimes envy them their life together and wish I could find for myself a lasting love like theirs. I aspire also to equal, in my profession, the accomplishments they've made in their own. They've afforded me this house to live in, no money in exchange, while I cobble together my career. A magnificent hundred-year-old house filled now with the sweet scent of mimosa. Blossoms drip from two giant trees in the backyard, each taller than the house, trees started from cuttings in the year Georgia and Alice were not married. Their generosity astounds me at times, so grand against my small, infrequent gestures. And yet, they are evil and the institution of marriage should be safeguarded against them.

LAST WINTER, A FEW days before Christmas, Alice phoned to ask if I could come over and help her carry some packages into the house. She had just returned from a trip to the mall and the back of her car was filled with bags and boxes. Two boxes were too heavy for her to handle. "These," she said, "the sales clerk had to help me carry them out." I pulled them from the trunk. One was a trash can; the other a Crock-Pot.

The day after Christmas, I asked Georgia what gifts she got. "A trash can," she said. I told her I had seen it, that, in fact, I had carried it in. She said it was the one she had really wanted: Tall, sleek, stainless steel, with a divider inside to separate dry trash from wet garbage. "I couldn't be happier," she said.

"Anything else?" I asked.

"Nope," she said.

"No Crock-Pot?"

"Oh. Alice bought that for herself." She laughed. "She thinks it will make it easier for her to get dinner on the table. Wait and see, she'll never use it."

At Easter, it was still in its box.

"Alice, why haven't you opened your Crock-Pot?" I asked.

"It isn't as easy as it looks," she said, and she handed me the free cookbook that came with it.

Crock-Pots had evolved. For one thing, they came in an army of sizes. In terms of finish, they had branched out from avocado, almond, and burnt orange as well. (Alice had chosen a stainless-steel finish. To match the trash can, I figured.) Today's were cheaper, too. Alice had paid ten dollars less than I had thirty years earlier. Her Crock-Pot was bigger and included a cookbook. I read some of the recipes. At first glance, they were confusing. Crock-Pots were no longer vehicles for simple stews. It appeared people used them now to prepare gourmet meals, and the recipes contained all kinds of caveats for adjusting ingredients according to the size Crock-Pot one was using. Too far one way and the resulting meal would be dreadfully dry, too far the other way, a culinary equivalent of the wetlands. It was a bit intimidating, but intriguing nonetheless.

"I'm going to have a dinner party in which all the courses are made in a Crock-Pot," I told Alice as I read the book.

"Can you really do that?" she asked.

"Yep," I said. "I'll need to borrow this book." I already had my eye on an appetizer. I turned to the section on desserts. "How do you feel about bread pudding?" I asked.

"Works for me," she said.

"When the time comes, I'll need to borrow your Crock-Pot, too," I told her. I already had three Crock-Pots of my own. My mother had given me all three: one when I moved into my first apartment; another when a cousin's wedding was canceled ("You might as well keep this," she said of the Crock-Pot she had already bought as a gift); the last when she decided to "downsize," explaining that the only meals she could make with her Crock-Pot were too big for two people. It was only her and my father left at home. I did not pursue the obvious: Why had she given a family-sized Crock-Pot to the only one of her children who lived alone?

By the time I get around to having my Crock-Pot dinner party, we Missourians will have probably already voted on whether we want to amend our constitution to assure that gay marriages will neither be made nor honored in the Show Me state. We've already passed a law making same-sex marriage illegal. But as we know, laws can be revoked. The constitutional amendment will offer added protection, that extra deadbolt on the door.

The last time a group of my friends who have been "not married" for many years came to my house for dinner, the conversation turned to high school. For better or worse, the older we get, the less often that happens. Three of the six women who were gathered around the table told stories about their first lesbian experiences. For better or worse, the older we get, the less often that happens as well. Each of these three women's first loves had been high-school teachers. Two of the teachers taught English; the third, gym. As far as I could tell, none of my friends had won her teacher over with a Crock-Pot.

With the exception of my sister, I have never told anyone—until now—about giving my high-school English teacher a Crock-Pot for her birthday. But today, when my friend called to tell me about the August vote, it made me think back to the first time in my life when it appeared that actions might be taken against me. A few months after she had invited me to dinner, my teacher called me aside after class. She had seen me driving past her house. Too often, she said. I had gotten my license by then, and my trips down her street had become more frequent. I never stopped or went to her door. But I drove down her street a lot, and she'd seen me. She'd noticed, too, she said that day, that we crossed paths quite a bit in the hallways between classes. Had I memorized her schedule so that I knew which class-rooms she would be in from one hour to the next? She was frightened by my behavior. Her boyfriend was concerned as well, she said. He considered me to be a stalker. If I kept it up, he might have to call the police.

I felt stunned and ashamed. Was I a stalker?

Since that night at her house, I had had lots of talks with her after class and after school, on the days I didn't have to get right home. I would never have been bold enough had she not given me the box of books that night after dinner, books by writers she said I might not find on my own. Sarah

Orne Jewett, Willa Cather, Djuna Barnes. None were obscure. In time, I would have found them. Gertrude Stein, Virginia Woolf. I did not realize until years later, however, that they were all lesbians. Had she been one herself? By giving me the books, was she declaring that part of her life to be over?

I had wanted to tell her things about myself, things I didn't even know yet. Up to then, however, I had managed only to talk about the Romantic poets and the other writers she told me to read. After the day that she expressed her and her boyfriend's concerns about me, I walked down different halls and drove down different streets. In time, I would learn there were others like me. For the most part, in my circle of friends, we have found ways to live the lives we've wanted. Others like us, I know, are not as lucky. In the short-term frenzy around Missouri's amendment, I think we will be defeated. I hope I am wrong. Someday, I want to witness the legal marriage ceremony of a couple like my friends Georgia and Alice.

Whoever the lucky pair, I won't give them a Crock-Pot for their wedding. That gift has bad karma to me.

Mrs. Register

BY MICHAEL PARKER

*. . . and yet, even as she arose, secure in her con-
victions, she was aware she had not
triumphed over them, nor destroyed them, nor
pacified them, but only pushed them away for a
little while, like nagging children.*
—EVAN CONNELL, *Mrs. Bridge*

I. BUSINESS MACHINES

In her junior year of high school, to give herself a break
from the stress and rigor of her precollegiate schedule,
Caroline "Cacky" Winston allowed herself a slide called
Business Machines. This was 1975, at Walter Page High
School in Greensboro, North Carolina, and the "business
machines" she was to study were even then in danger of ob-
solescence: the ten-key adding machine, the stenograph,
the dictaphone. That the machines would like as not be

replaced by more progressive technology before Caroline graduated from college mattered not at all to her, as she was taking the class ironically.

She wasn't the only one. Two seats behind her sat a boy named Sean Underwood. Though he was an inch or so shorter than Caroline, not usually something she would tolerate in a boy, her opinion changed once they were paired up to work together on the dictaphone. He was marvelously witty in a way she'd seen in men only in the movies. He didn't seem like he was from Greensboro. He was on the swim team, and played the viola in the orchestra, but he had long feathered hair and dressed like he was in a glam rock band: tight shirts with three-quarter-length sleeves, jeans with wide-belled bottoms. Again, not usually Caroline's thing—she went more for the preppie type—but within days they were hanging out together after class, and within a couple weeks she was talking to Sean all night on the phone, neglecting her friends, her calculus homework, her family. Mostly they talked about other kids at school, though they also talked about what they wanted after Page High School. Sean wanted to be an architect. She had seen him drawing plans during Business Machines. Caroline wanted to go to law school, though she did not want to come back to Greensboro and set up a shingle with her father, which was her father's dream. She wanted to move to New Orleans, and live above a narrow brick street in a wide, slope-floored apartment with wrought-iron balconies and caged birds. She didn't think she wanted to get married, really.

Oh, come on, Cacky, Sean could have said, you'll be married before you're twenty-five. This was what her boyfriend, Kevin, said all the time. He wanted to marry her after they graduated from Wake Forest. He had it all planned out. Currently she was taking a break from Kevin, who spent much of his time slamming his locker door whenever one of Caroline's friends passed close by, so that she'd hear how upset he was. Word reached him that she was spending all her time with Sean.

"I guess I don't have to worry about you leaving me for that guy," Kevin would say to her on the phone.

"Why would that be?"

"What a lame-ass. He wears platform shoes. It's like he's trying out for Mott the Hoople."

She would hang up and call Sean. And he would talk to her about her life (though only guardedly about his) and he would take her seriously in a way that no boy ever had before, and he was so witty, so adept with words and phrases, and it had never occurred to her how sexy words could be. In English, Mrs. Cushman made them read *As I Lay Dying*, and Caroline sort of skimmed a lot of it until she got to the part where the dead woman said that words were "just a shape to fill a lack." Caroline underlined this phrase three times and drew an arrow out to the margin where neatly she pinned three exclamation points, and before the ink had dried she was on the phone to Sean to share with him how mysteriously hollow these words made her feel.

2. "FAME" BY DAVID BOWIE

A new dance club had opened downtown. Disco had hit, and Caroline wanted to dance. Kevin did not dance, and none of Caroline's friends were ingenious enough to procure fake IDs, so she asked Sean, who she knew went to Phases every weekend, to take her. Caroline told her parents she was spending the night with a friend. Phases stayed open until six on Saturday nights. They planned to dance all night long, go somewhere and watch the sun come up, then have breakfast. On the way to the club, they talked about Kevin, why Caroline stayed with him.

"I don't know, I guess he's just convenient," she said. "Oh my God, I didn't mean that. He's really nice, Sean."

"I'm sure," said Sean.

"It's just, he doesn't really like to talk very much. I mean, I'm not even sure he knows how to."

They laughed about this, and other things, and at the club Sean somehow found a bartender who would serve them drinks, and he seemed to know half the people there. They set themselves up in a dark corner among a large group of drinkers, mostly college students, mostly guys. Caroline got quickly and loudly drunk. She dragged Sean out on the dance floor for every KC and the Sunshine hit, nearly every other song. She smiled at everyone and banged on the glass of the DJ booth, begging the oblivious, head-phoned DJ to please please play Parliament's "Flashlight." It grew late and fuzzy. Caroline felt queasy, all the drinks, the swirling lights, the strobes; she leaned against Sean for a slow dance to "Behind Closed Doors," by Charlie Rich, which Sean's corner crowd inexplicably knew all the words to, and sang loudly in an exaggerated twang: ". . . Makes me glad to be a man / because no-one knows what goes on behind closed doors." Then they were dancing faster, to "Fame," by David Bowie, and Caroline had her arms around Sean's neck and her mouth against his. Drunkenly she pushed her tongue into his mouth. She felt his teeth clamp together. She heard him say her name. She shook her head petulantly and dragged him over to a corner and pushed herself against him as David Bowie repeated, "What's your game what's your game," and Sean kept saying her name and said he just wanted to hold her, but she did not stop trying to kiss him until she looked over at Sean's friends, all guys now, and saw how they were laughing, and she stood back and looked at Sean.

"My God."

"I wanted to tell you," he said. "I'm sorry, I just didn't know how."

But she did not hear him. She vomited all over his platform shoes.

3. SOCIAL PROBLEMS

In her third year at Chapel Hill, Caroline, exhausted by all the English classes she was taking because it had been suggested as a wiser path to law school than your basic prelaw curriculum, took a course called Social Problems. The class was full of fraternity brothers of her boyfriend, Roger, and it reminded her, in title and content, of Business Machines, which made her miss Sean. He was down in Savannah at art school, studying design. They talked less and less those days—it had been a few months, longest time ever—though they always got together over Christmas break and summer.

Call Sean, Caroline wrote on her notebook in Social Problems, as a boy she knew slightly, one of Roger's fraternity brothers, stood up to give his oral report on Homosexuality and Other Deviant Sexual Behaviors.

Homosexuality, Caroline wrote in her notebook.

Well of course it's a sin, says so in the Bible, the boy said, not even to mention a crime, punishable in most states, including the one we're sitting in, by incarceration. Several times the boy mentioned that he was giving an oral report, putting undue and dramatic emphasis on the word oral, and toward the back of the room there was muffled snorting among a few of his frat brothers.

"In my *oral* report I would like to catalog some names by which males of the homosexual persuasion are casually referred to: fags, fairies, queers, queens, butt blasters, pansies, nancy girls, cocksuckers . . ."

Caroline looked at the professor. He sat in the corner, taking notes on the boy's oral report, a scribe, impassive. No one else in the room seemed to be paying any attention save the back row, who, during the question-and-answer portion of the report, pelted him with silly questions (where did you do your research?). Caroline thought of how, after that night at Phases, when Sean admitted he was gay, she never talked to him about it, really. She avoided it by never sharing with Sean any details of her own romantic life. Well, after all, he would not care for Roger, and she couldn't imagine liking any boy he was with. It was too, um, weird.

The boy sat down. The professor got up and thanked the boy, as if what he'd shared was helpful. Caroline felt the blood flushing her face; embarrassed, she looked down at her notebook, upon which she'd written:

Social Problems

Call Sean

Homosexuality

4 · LOVE AND MARRIAGE

The summer after she graduated from college, Caroline married Roger Register. A half hour before she was to walk down the aisle, she shocked her bridesmaids by sending them all out of the Sunday-school classroom where they had set up camp and fetching her sister to find Sean and bring him to her.

After they hugged and had a little cry, Caroline told Sean how great he looked. He'd moved to New York, entered grad school in architecture; his hair was shorter and his shoulders were wider and he was tanned from weekends spent at an island time-share with his city friends.

Caroline's mother knocked on the door.

"Go away, Mother," called Caroline. She said to Sean,

"This room smells like chalk dust. Now, whenever I smell chalk dust, I'll think about marriage."

She was joking, but not really. Sean said, "It reminds me of all the Bible stories I used to know and seem to have forgotten."

"You remember everything," she said. "You'll remember this, way longer than I will. In a couple of days, the whole thing will be a blur."

"Same for everyone who goes through it, I'm sure." He took her hand and assured her it would soon be over.

"Did you ever want to get married, Sean?"

"You mean do I ever wish I wasn't gay?"

That wasn't what she meant, really, but she could see how he could interpret it that way.

"Of course I have. But what can I do about it? Lean into it, I guess. Let's not talk about that, though."

"We never really have before."

"True enough, but the natives are getting restless." He nodded over his shoulder at the knockings, light but persistent.

"That's Mother's knock," said Caroline. "I bet I'll grow up to knock just like that on my daughter's wedding day." The thought of her own daughter holed up in a chalkdusty classroom with a male friend in the final, sweetly special moments before her wedding—moments that should be shared with family—disturbed her so much that she came close to asking Sean to leave. But instead she asked him if he'd seen Roger.

"Sure," he said. "We talked."

Caroline searched his face for signs of disapproval. She knew he would support her, even though it was clear that Sean made Roger uncomfortable, and she knew that Sean, as perceptive as he was, picked up on Roger's discomfort.

"Well, anyway, be glad you never have to bother with all this," she said, rustling her ridiculously expensive dress.

"Oh, I don't know. Seems pretty wonderful to me."

"You mean you'd want to?"

"For the right fellow, I guess."

The door swung open. The look on Caroline's mother's face so horrified Caroline that her own face mirrored the anxiety. She saw that Sean thought she was horrified by what he'd said, and she wanted to apologize, but he smiled thinly, kissed her cheek, and was gone before she could say anything.

5. BARBECUE

Oddly enough, it was not Caroline but Roger who went to law school and ended up joining her father's firm after they moved back to Greensboro. Caroline went to work running the Episcopal Church preschool, a job which reeked of chalk dust, though her prediction to Sean that morning at her wedding—that chalk dust would thereafter remind her of marriage—turned out not to be true. She never thought of marriage. She loved her husband well enough, but she never thought much about her love for him, and in time it seemed to her that if she had to think about it, well, it couldn't very well be love.

She had three girls in a row, and she stayed home with them until the youngest, Ann-Hutchinson, was a junior in high school. At forty-five, just to get out of the house, Caroline went to work part time for a friend, Becky, who owned a tiny store on State Street which sold coffee, tea, and gourmet pasta.

One afternoon she was minding the store when Sean appeared on the sidewalk outside. He rapped on the platform to get her attention, then mashed his face against it like a child.

"I didn't know you were home," she said after she hugged him and poured him a cup of coffee. In the past few years they'd mostly fallen out of touch. Christmas cards, a phone call, or quick drink when Sean came home to see his parents, who had moved into a retirement home. He'd left New York long ago, first for San Diego, then Spain, where he'd lived for ten years with a man named Guillermo. Caroline had never met Guillermo, or any of Sean's friends.

"How long are you in town for?"

Sean told her that he'd bought his parents house in Fisher Park and was renovating it. He said he planned on staying.

Caroline's squeals brought Becky out of her office. When Becky was safely out of earshot, Caroline said, "As much as I will love having you, I have to ask . . ."

"Yeah, I know, why would I want to move back here? I don't know, I miss it. I like the rhythm down here. I like the way people talk. I don't see why I have to keep exiling myself to places that are fine for a while, even wonderful—I can't really complain about Barcelona or Manhattan—but don't feel like home to me. Plus, I miss the barbecue."

Caroline said, "So is Guillermo coming too?"

"You never could pronounce his name," said Sean. "Yes, he's coming too."

"Well, there are a lot of Spanish-speakers in the area now," said Caroline. "I believe most of them work in the chicken plants."

Sean smiled and asked after her children, and they made a date to play tennis later that week. When he left, Caroline moved to the window to watch him walk down the street. He stopped to talk to a handsome, dark-haired man leaning against a clean white rental car.

Becky was right behind her, asking who Sean was.

"An old friend."

Becky said that Caroline didn't seem too happy to see him, and Caroline replied that she was, in fact, terribly happy to see him, and she told Becky she needed to leave early to take Ann-Hutchinson to the orthodontist and made up her mind, at that moment, to quit this silly part-time job.

6. POWER FORWARD

Every year Roger and Caroline hosted a party during the ACC basketball tournament. This year Roger had rented a wide-screen, high-definition television set and pushed it against the built-in-bookcases in the den. To Caroline it was a sight. She thought it made her home look like a sports bar. She might as well serve chicken wings. She'd fought with Roger about it, and about the guest list.

"You're inviting Sean and his friend?" Roger asked.

"Guillermo," said Caroline, manipulating her l's the way Sean did. Roger always called Guillermo "his friend." She'd invited them to parties before, and Roger was polite but distant. He was friendlier to Guillermo than to Sean, probably because Guillermo was foreign and Roger assumed he understood only half of what was said to him. Also, Roger had never gone out of his way to get to know Caroline's friends from before they met. Once, she had called him on it and he said he was a very busy man and it seemed to him an inefficient use of his time to try and play catch up. I'd lose for sure at that game, he said. Roger had one subject which he talked to Sean about: city planning. Many times Caroline had told Roger that Sean was an architect, not a city planner. Once, Roger changed the subject briefly to his suspicion that they might need to put in a French drain due to wetness in the basement, and what did Sean think about that? Sean gave a guarded opinion, stressing that he wasn't a landscape architect, after which Roger, who had been appointed to a municipal committee on development and zoning issues, switched the subject back to city planning.

"I don't know, Cacky. I don't think they'd be real comfortable. It's a basketball tournament."

"Guillermo won't come. He's not interested in basketball. But Sean's obsessed with it. He already told me he's dying to watch the game with someone who knows the difference between a point guard and a power forward."

"You don't think he's just being polite?"

"Sean is not that polite when it comes to doing things he's not interested in."

"Well, in my observation, that's characteristic."

"Of what?"

"Of the gays. They can be real selfish people."

"Roger, what on earth are you saying?"

"Most of them are very . . ." Roger looked at his wife, and then at his watch, as if he did not have time to explain this idea to Caroline, who he was pretty sure wouldn't have understood anyway. Caroline knew that Roger felt she was, in general, oblivious.

The house filled with their friends. Women gathered in the kitchen, drinking wine or cans of beer wrapped in napkins, and the men hovered around the awful television set, swearing mildly under their breath. Caroline moved between the two rooms, freshening drinks, refilling snack trays. She noticed that Roger and Sean were talking nearly every other time she entered the den.

After the game was over, Sean came to find her to say good-bye.

"I wish Guillermo would have come," she said.

"He'd have stayed in the kitchen, drinking wine and swapping recipes with the girls."

This made her blush. Was Sean the "man"? The idea bothered her more than she wanted it to. She could not get it out of her mind. It did not help when Roger, a little tipsy, helping her clean up, said, "You know it's the damndest thing, Cack. Your friend Sean knows more about ACC basketball than anyone I've ever met."

• • •

7 · LOVE AND MARRIAGE

On the news the mayor of San Francisco appeared nightly, smiling into the camera while behind him the hallways of the courthouse clogged with lines of homosexual couples waiting to be married.

Now that Ann-Hutchinson was out of the house, Caroline and Roger ate dinner every night in front of the television. Roger liked to watch Dan Rather and then, while Caroline fetched dessert, the first two rounds of *Jeopardy!* He always excused himself before Final Jeopardy as he complained that the questions were impossibly difficult, that it was rigged to make people lose all the money they'd earned in the preliminary rounds.

"Looks like he's up for reelection," said Roger, pointing a forked piece of chicken at the mayor of San Francisco.

Caroline thought the mayor awfully handsome. She said he seemed a little young to be a mayor of a huge city, and that he appeared to be such a nice man.

"Nice men don't get reelected," said Roger. "He's just playing to his constituency."

"Why do so many gay people live in San Francisco?"

Roger ignored her to stare at the television screen, which pictured two elderly women—Caroline's mother's age—holding flowers and kissing. She knew that Roger had heard her and she knew he'd answer in time, whether he had an answer or not.

"It's like the Mexicans who come up here and get work in the chicken plants," he said. "All it takes is one of them calling his buddies back in Cancún or wherever."

"You think all gay people know each other?"

Roger looked at her, then at the television screen. Calmly he said, "I hope your buddy Sean and his friend aren't thinking of tying the knot."

"Why do you care?"

He shrugged. "Anyway, it'll never hold up in court." He went into a lengthy explanation of the legal issues involved. She held his gaze, forcing him to finish, to be thorough. She was interested, and she could tell he was waiting for her interest to wane and for her to cut her eyes to a commercial and say, "Oh well, it's certainly complicated," and disappear to get him a fruit cup or, these days, a low-carb Popsicle, since they were both on Atkins.

"Those seem to me man-made laws," said Caroline.

Roger looked perturbed. She never argued with him about the law.

"There are plenty of God-made ones," he said. "They're in the Bible. People are quoting them right and left in the letters to the editor."

"Well, you know, maybe the Bible's a little out of touch."

"Ha!" said Roger. "Tell that to the Christian Right."

"Okay, I will," she said. "I'll write a letter to the editor and say just that."

"I wouldn't if I were you," said Roger.

The only reply she could think of was something she used to say, under her breath, to her mother when her mother used this phrase: but you're not me. Instead of saying something so silly, she got up to get them both Popsicles.

That night she lay awake thinking of her own wedding day, of how she'd banished all her bridesmaids and brought Sean in to spend that last half hour with her. At the time it had seemed like the most important day of her life. Now it seemed like just another Saturday afternoon. She hated Saturdays—the hum of the refrigerator, the commercials blaring between plays of the ball games Roger watched, the weedeaters and leafblowers—it was always so loud, and she was always so sleepy. Now that she wasn't working, she couldn't bring herself to take a nap, for it did not seem she'd earned it.

Well, as she understood it, these gay weddings weren't very ceremonious, or reserved for Saturday afternoons. It seemed to Caroline that you just stood in line forever, and according to Roger there was a large chance that it wouldn't mean very much at all, in the long run. All in all, it seemed a good thing that Sean stay away from San Francisco.

8. ANSWERING MACHINE

But Sean did not stay away from marriage. San Francisco was no longer performing the gay weddings, but a place in Oregon was, and a week after her conversation with Roger, Sean called to say that he and Guillermo had booked a flight for Portland and were leaving in the morning.

"Oh my land," she said. This was a phrase her mother had

used when she didn't know what else to say. What did it even mean? She didn't have any land. A song from elementary school came into her head—"This land is your land, this land is my land"—and she tried to remember the next lines as Sean filled her in on the details of his trip.

"I'm so happy for you," she said. But she didn't feel very happy, really. She felt sad and preoccupied, desperate to remember the next line of that song, as if it was more crucial than the most important news Sean had ever shared with her. There was something she knew but had forgotten, or could not articulate.

She thought of what Roger would say when she told him. She remembered her conversation with him about this topic when it was only hypothetical. The arguments, the issues— legal ones, moral ones—struck her as irrelevant now that Sean was on the line, announcing his plans. It seemed to her that everyone—the lawmakers, the elected officials, the fundamentalist Christians, the gay rights activists, the Socialists—was appropriating the issue for their own agenda. Well, she wasn't exactly selfless in her approach, for at that moment, the whole thing seemed about her. Fear and hollowness and desire for words that were more than a shape to fill a lack.

She knew that if one of her daughters took her aside and confessed her homosexuality, she would say, Honey, I love you and will support you but I think it's just tragic that you can't marry and have children, as that part of my life has been the most rewarding. But that was not exactly true.

Nights in front of the television, Dan Rather in the background, Roger talked to her about the wet basements, French drains. Her marriage had been characterized by a nearly manic zeal for domestic details—housekeeping, money, retirement—in contrast to those moments she shared with Sean, those laid-bare emotional discussions when she felt understood and appreciated, when she gave good advice, as opposed to the distantly maternal, I'm-staying-out-of-it roteness she doled out to her own daughters. Roger never sought her advice on anything. Sometimes he would have a bad day, or his back would be bothering him, and she would try to comfort him, but he would not let her.

She kept Sean going with questions but the more he

talked, the more detached and miserable she felt. Then it came to her: they would need a witness. Sean had been, in a way, the most important person at her wedding. She needed him to know who she was. She needed Roger and the rest of her friends to know who she was not.

"When do we leave?" she asked.

"We?"

"You'll need a witness," she said. "That's how a civil ceremony works, honey."

"That's sweet, Cack. But we'll just nab someone off the street. I'm sure they'll be enough homos standing around, given what's going on out there."

Caroline hated it when Sean used words like "homo," or "queer." She bit her tongue and said, "You will not either ask a total stranger to witness your wedding. If you're going to do this thing, you're going to do it right. Now if I'm going to get a seat on that plane, I need to get cracking. You need to tell me what time it leaves."

After another minute of back and forth, Sean gave in to her demands. She wrote down the flight information and hung up the phone feeling giddy, but it took her a half hour to work up the nerve to call Roger at work. She was pacing the house, carrying the phone around, when Sean called back.

"I discussed it with Guillermo. We both think you're so sweet to offer, it's really really nice, but . . . "

Caroline sucked in her bottom lip to keep from crying. Why would they want her there?

"Of course I understand," she said. "I'd only be in the way."

"Oh it's not that, it's just . . . " but Caroline spared him the indignity of having to explain with a comment about someone needing to take care of Roger.

That night at dinner, Caroline insisted they eat at the table.

"I want to watch the news," said Roger.

"You can watch it by yourself," she said. "It's uncivilized, slouching in front of the television every night with your plate propped up on a pillow."

"What's gotten into you?"

She felt her mouth tighten. She could not tell him she was just tired, for he would ask her what did she do all day to make her so tired? Well, no, he would never say that, but he would think it. The truth was, she'd felt unsettled all day. She wasn't at all angry at Sean for turning her down—she was glad he'd said no. She was mad at him for making her feel so inarticulate, so unable to communicate to him what she felt about marriage. She remembered fighting the same impulse when her own daughters married, but given who they were, how they were raised, well, they had to get married. Why did Sean have to get married? It wasn't a question of benefits, as it was for so many of them. He had money. He was happy with Guillermo. Really, this whole thing had turned into a huge mess. She had never felt such turmoil. She felt Sean was letting her down, making a point that was finally rather pointless. What was the point?

The next evening she was cooking dinner when the phone rang. Afraid it might be Sean, she let the machine pick up. Sean's voice came on, and he said, simply, "Well, I'm married. I don't know if it means anything legally or not. I guess we'll see. I love you. Talk to you when I get back."

Roger was in the laundry room, cleaning his golf shoes. He came into the kitchen just as Sean hung up.

"Who was that?"

"Sean."

"Did I hear him say he's married?"

"Yes, that's what he said."

"Hmmm," said Roger. He looked at her, then grabbed a paper towel from the dispenser and went back to the laundry room carrying his golf shoes, but his hum remained, growing louder until, finally, it was absorbed by the refrigerator, the television, weedeaters and leafblowers, all the annoying noises of her Saturday afternoons. The hum continued even after Caroline, to distract herself from it, had an idea: she would throw them a party upon their return. It was the least she could do. She wasn't sure what would give her more pleasure—planning the menu or imagining the looks on her friends' faces when they opened the envelope, expecting an invitation for Derby Day drinks, and read the names of the betrothed, which she would pay to have embossed in gold, just like a real wedding.

Double Standards

BY DAN SAVAGE

WE WERE HAVING DINNER with some friends, a nice couple, around our age, good parents to two girls. Our kids were tearing around in the yard and the adults were well into our third bottle of wine when the conversation turned to sex. We knew the wife was relatively young and sexually inexperienced when she married—she had confided that in us the first time we'd been over to dinner, a year before. She had always felt as if she'd missed out, she told us. She never really had any sexual adventures; she had never done anything she regretted or looked back on and thought, "Wow! Was that me?!?"

We were the only gay couple she knew, me and my boyfriend, and she had been initiating slightly awkward conversations about sex with us ever since we met when our kids started attending the same school. She seemed hung up on our gayness but not in a bad way. She seemed jealous. She assumed that, because we were gay, we had both had wild sexual experiences, the kind of adventures she had missed out on, and after two or three glasses of wine she would start demanding the details. Tonight she wanted to talk about infidelity.

"Have you ever cheated on Terry?" she asked me.

I looked at Terry and made my "am I allowed to answer this question truthfully?" face. He nodded his head to one side, making his "go-ahead and tell her what she wants to know" face.

"Sure, I've cheated on Terry," I said, after checking to make sure the kids were all out of earshot. "But only in front of him."

She laughed and looked at me, then Terry, then me again. Were we joking? I shrugged my shoulders. It wasn't a joke, the shrug said. I had "cheated" on Terry—but only in front of him, only with his permission, only with someone we both liked and trusted, only when we were in one city and our son was in another. So, yes, we've had a threeway—actually we've had a couple, and while threeways barely register on the kink-o-meter anymore, they're considered the absolute height of kink for people like us—for parents, I mean, not for gay people. As parents we're not really supposed to be having sex with each other anymore, much less having sex with someone else.

She demanded the details but I would only give her a basic outline. One was a nice French guy who looked like Tom Cruise. The other was an ex-boyfriend of mine, a Microsoft millionaire who spent hundreds of thousands of dollars building a "playroom" in his basement—a kind of sex-toy wonderland. Terry wanted to see this playroom for himself and so we went over for dinner . . . and one thing led to another . . .

We emphasized that we regarded threeways the same way Bill Clinton regarded abortion: They're best when they're safe, legal, and rare. Really rare—two in ten years? We get to vote for president more often than we have threeways.

When we were done her eyes widened and she leaned in and grabbed my arm.

"That's wonderful," she said, a little too loudly. "I would love to have a threeway. Or an affair." She pronounced the word "ah-fay-yah," for comic effect. "An ah-fay-yah, I think, would be better than a thu-ree-waya. I don't think I would want my husband to know the details."

She said all of this in front of her husband, of course, who laughed at what he believed was a joke.

A COUPLE OF BIZARRE double standards have been getting a lot of press since those "unelected, activist judges" in Massachusetts, as George W. Bush likes to call them (should George W. Bush really be pointing fingers at unelected public officials?), and the mayor of San Francisco kick-started the debate on gay marriage.

The double standard promoted by opponents of gay marriage relentlessly—and attacked just as relentlessly by supporters—is that marriage is about having children. Since gays and lesbians can't have children, according to religious conservatives, we shouldn't be allowed to marry. It has been almost comically easy to punch holes in this argument. Not all married straight couples can have children (the elderly, the sterile); many straight couples who can have children choose not to. And it's not exactly a secret that thousands of gay and lesbian couples have had children or plan to have children through adoption or artificial insemination. If marriage is about children, how is it that childless straight couples can marry but same-sex couples with children cannot?

By promoting this double standard, social conservatives have unwittingly exposed the shocking truth about marriage in America today: The institution of marriage, as currently practiced, is terrifically hard to define. Marriage is whatever two straight people say it is. Kids? Optional. Honor? Let's hope so. Till death do us part? There's a 50/50 chance of that. Obey? Only if you're a female Southern Baptist. Modern marriage can be sacred (church, family, preacher), or profane (Vegas, strangers, Elvis). What makes a straight couple married—in their own eyes, in the eyes of the state— is their professed love, a license issued by a state, and the couple's willingness to commit to each other publicly. How a straight married couple chooses to express their love, exactly what it is they're committing to, is entirely up to them. It's not up to the state, their reproductive systems, or even the church that solemnizes their vows.

This is the reason so many defenders of "traditional

marriage" sputtered their way through their appearances on *Nightline* and the Sunday morning news programs. Traditional marriage is just one option among many these days. A religious straight couple can have a big church wedding and kids and the wife can submit to the husband and they can stay married until death parts them—provided that's what they both want. Or a couple of straight atheists can get married in a tank full of dolphins and never have kids and treat each other as equals and split up if they decide their marriage isn't working out—again, if that's what they both want. (It should be pointed out, however, that a religious couple is likelier to divorce than a couple who marry in a tank full of dolphins.) The problem for opponents of gay marriage isn't that gay people are trying to redefine marriage but that straight people have redefined marriage to a point that it no longer makes any sense to exclude gay couples. Gay people can love, gay people can commit. Some of us even have children. So why can't we get married?

But supporters of gay marriage have been peddling a double standard of their own, one that's just as easy to punch holes in.

Gene Robinson, the openly gay Episcopal bishop of New Hampshire, told the Associated Press that "it serves the common good also to support same-gender couples who wish to pledge fidelity, monogamy, and lifelong commitment." On *Larry King Live,* Gavin Newsom, the heterosexual mayor of San Francisco, claimed that he was only "advancing the bond of love and monogamy." On CNN's *NewsNight with Aaron Brown,* conservative commentator and early gay marriage advocate Andrew Sullivan described the gay marriage movement as "a very conservative thing. . . . We're arguing for the same conservative values of family and responsibility and monogamy that everybody else is." In the *Washington Times,* Democratic consultant Michael Goldman encouraged Democrats to defend civil unions for gays by saying, "[They're] about two things, which I favor—monogamy and accountability."

Excuse me? Monogamy does not define marriage any more than the presence of children does. Straight couples don't have to be monogamous to be married or married to be monogamous. Monogamy isn't compulsory and its absence doesn't invalidate a marriage. There are hundreds of thousands of heterosexual married couples involved in the organized swinging movement and God only knows how many disorganized swingers are out there. Married straight couples are presumed to be monogamous until proven otherwise, of course, and that assumption serves as a powerful inducement to be (or appear to be) monogamous. Even most swinging couples prefer to be seen as monogamous by friends, family, and associates. But as with children, monogamy is optional. It's up to each individual couple to decide for themselves if monogamy is central to their commitment.

By promoting the idea that monogamy is central to marriage and that all gay couples who want to marry want to be monogamous, supporters of gay marriage have created a double standard of our own—one that opponents of gay marriage can poke holes in pretty easily. Just as supporters of gay marriage can produce gay and lesbian couples with children, opponents of gay marriage won't have to search too hard to find non-monogamous gay couples among the thousands of same-sex couples who wed in San Francisco, before the courts called a halt to same-sex marriages there, and who are marrying now in Massachusetts.

Indeed, my own relationship presents a tough case for

opponents and supporters of gay marriage alike. My boyfriend and I have a child; we're thinking of adopting another. If children are the gold standard, we should be married. But if monogamy is the gold standard, then the couple of threeways we admit to having disqualify us.

All sorts of nightmare scenarios play out in peoples' minds when a male couple—particularly one with kids—admits to being non-monogamous. While married couples are presumed to be sober monogamists until proven otherwise, non-monogamous gay male couples are presumed to be reckless sluts until proven otherwise. So once again and this time for the record: My boyfriend and I don't hang out in sleazy bars at all hours, we don't have threeways with men we've met on the Internet, and neither of us is willing to take irrational risks for the sake of the next orgasm. Like a huge number of straight couples, we have an understanding. "Cheating" is permissible under a few tightly controlled and highly unlikely circumstances; finally, all outside sexual contact has to be very safe—indeed, it has to be hyper safe, almost comically safe. We've never done anything, nor would we ever do anything, that would put our child at risk.

(There will be no *Kramer vs. Kramer* moments—i.e., no strange adults wandering nude through our house in the middle of the night.) For all intents and purposes, the limits we've placed on outside sexual contact have resulted in a sort of de facto monogamy. In the ten years we've been together the planets have aligned on a couple of occasions. We're more non-monogamous in theory than in practice.

So why not keep our mouths shut and let people assume we're monogamous? For the most part that's what we do—gay or straight, it's what most couples with understandings about outside sexual contact do. Like most long-term couples, my boyfriend and I don't rub our friends' and neighbors' noses in the details of our private life—unless we're pressed, of course, by drunk straight friends. But sexual honesty is a hard habit to break. Once you've told people that you're gay, telling them that you're non-monogamous seems like pretty small beans. And with so many supporters of gay marriage busily promoting a double standard about monogamy, I felt like at least one gay couple who wanted to marry but didn't want to be monogamous should speak up.

We want equal marriage rights, after all, not the right to be held to a higher standard than straight people hold themselves—on being parents or being strictly monogamous.

THERE ARE TWO LINES of thought when it comes to allowing gay men to marry: marriage will change us, making us more monogamous, or we will change marriage, making it less monogamous. On *Talk of the Nation*, Jonathan Katz, executive coordinator of Larry Kramer Initiative for Lesbian and Gay Studies at Yale University, made the case for the latter. "[Monogamy is] one of the pillars of heterosexual marriage and perhaps its key source of trauma," Katz said. "Could it be that the inclusion of lesbian and gay same-sex marriage may, in fact, sort of de-center the notion of monogamy and allow the prospect that marriage need not be an exclusive sexual relationship among people?" In his book *Gay Marriage: Why It Is Good for Gays, Good for Straights, and Good for America*, Jonathan Rauch writes that "once gay couples are equipped with the entitlements and entanglements of legal marriage, same-sex relationships will continue to move toward both durability and exclusivity."

I think it's possible that Katz and Rauch are both right. If gay marriage is legalized once and for all, not all gay married couples will choose to be monogamous, just as not all straight couples choose to be monogamous. I would guess that married gay male couples will be non-monogamous at higher rates than married straight couples. (Married lesbians, studies show, will be monogamous at higher rates than straight or gay male couples.) But with marriage comes the assumption of monogamy and, if a couple has kids, a host of logistical and ethical roadblocks to being non-monogamous. Marriage may not transform gay men into models of monogamous behavior, but marriage and family life will nudge us in that direction, moving us toward durability and exclusivity. But as gay people tend to be more open about the details of our sexual lives, gay couples with "understandings" about outside sexual contact are likelier to be honest and, therefore, likelier to promote the notion that marriage need not be an exclusive sexual relationship.

Ultimately gay people only want what straight people have already got: the right for each couple to define marriage for themselves. Kids? No kids? Sexually exclusive? Open relationship? A lifetime? A starter marriage? Other peoples' standards—particularly their double standards—do not bind straight couples. They shouldn't bind gay ones either.

OH, AND SPEAKING OF TRAUMA . . .

I agree with Jonathan Katz when he says that monogamy is "one of the pillars of heterosexual marriage and perhaps its key source of trauma." It's almost impossible for two people to be all things to each other sexually and the expectation that two people can or should be all things to each other sexually—that they should never find another person attractive or act on that attraction—does a great deal of harm. Human beings didn't evolve to be monogamous and everything from divorce rates to recent impeachment proceedings prove, I think, that the expectation of life-long monogamy places an incredible strain on a marriage. Being monogamous is hard work; it's not natural (even disgraced virtuecrat William Bennett concedes this point!) and it doesn't come easily to human beings or very many other mammals. But our concept of love and marriage has as its foundation not only the expectation of monogamy but the idea that where there's love, monogamy should be easy and joyful.

Since I don't demand or expect complete fidelity from my boyfriend, I'm not traumatized when he finds another guy attractive; nor have I been traumatized when he's acted on an attraction to someone else—provided, of course, that all of our rules and regulations have been followed to the letter, as they always have been. Unlike a lot of straight couples, we've found a way to make our desire for others a non-issue in our relationship. Indeed, as most heterosexual swingers report, the few times we've had sex with other guys have actually enhanced the sex we have with each other. Far from tearing us apart, the times we've had sex with another man—the times we've had sexual adventures together—have renewed and refreshed our intimate life.

All of this came rushing into my head when our friends—the straight couple with the two girls—announced that they were separating. The wife wants to have her sexual adventures, the ones she missed out on by marrying so young. Since there's no room in their marriage for non-monogamy—since they can't go on a sexual adventure together—their marriage has to go. It's a shame, isn't it? A little non-monogamy could have saved their marriage, I'm convinced, but they can't conceive of being together, of being married, without being sexually exclusive. So the desire to have sex with someone else, to finally go and have that ah-fay-yah, means their marriage has to end.

It's too bad for those two girls that their parents aren't gay men, isn't it?

Stanley Karenina

BY JIM GRIMSLEY

HAPPY MARRIAGES ARE all alike. Each unhappy marriage is unhappy in its own way.

When Stanley married Bob, swearing before God to love, honor, and obey, until death do them part, they were each as sincere as men can be. Men, gay or straight, always are sincere to the best of their abilities, which often are not great.

When marrying Stanley, Bob felt completely convinced that he was on the right path, finally, after a lot of waffling and hiding from himself. Bob had met someone whom he felt he could love forever. Like so many people, Bob had felt this way before.

For instance, Bob had been completely convinced of his own correctness when he married Irene right after college, too. He would come to think of Irene as his first wife, and

Stanley as his second. He married Irene in a Methodist Church and Stanley in a Unitarian Fellowship Center. In neither of Bob's marriages was he the write-your-own-vows type. He liked the standard words that he had heard all his life on television and in the movies. But when he married Irene, he didn't know he was gay. Or he knew, and he pretended it would go away, like a prolonged head cold. So later he would think that his marriage to Irene did not really count.

Stanley had never been married. He had been too aware of the tragic consequences of a bad choice, such as the death of Anna Karenina. He had longed for a love for which he would fling himself under a train without a second thought, but only when he met Bob did he feel such a stirring. Bob being married, at first Stanley decided this feeling was the recurrence of his old need for approval from straight men, the issue that had kept him in years of group therapy. The two men met at a racetrack. Bob introduced himself to Stanley while they stood in line to bet on a filly ridden by a Russian jockey. The odds were long, ten to one or more. The filly broke her leg on the homestretch. Bob and Stanley were watching each other as the horse collapsed on the track, shuddering and heaving in the dry red dirt. Bob signaled to Stanley and they walked away together.

Which kind of marriage is the sacred one, the kind Bob had to Irene or the kind Bob had to Stanley?

When Bob was married to Irene, she thought they had a pretty good sex life. A pretty good sex life was all she wanted. Neither of them had ever been enthusiastic about copulation, even in college, when they'd made a kind of silent agreement to have sex in order to feel more comfortable in other social settings, where it was helpful no longer to be virgins. They attempted to enjoy their activities but mostly finished as quickly as possible. By the time they were married they had grown used to having sex on occasion and even enjoying it, though Irene's orgasms often disturbed Bob.

Stanley and Bob, after a staggering amount of intercourse in the early months of their relationship, settled down to much the same pattern.

Bob had cheated on Irene a number of times during their years together, and never told her about any of the times this happened, and never got caught. He chose both men and women for his betrayals. Far from cleaving only unto Irene, he cleaved unto almost anybody he met.

When Bob and Stanley got married, however, Stanley was the first to cheat. He did it with an old boyfriend in the bathroom during the wedding reception. Later he would tell himself he succumbed to temptation because he was frightened of commitment.

Both Irene and Stanley were scarred by the divorce of their own parents, though they never discussed this with one another the few times they actually met. Bob's parents' marriage had lasted fifty years, marked by the fact that neither parent would leave the company of the other and that neither ever spoke to the other except to fill the most basic of needs, such as locating the remote control for the television or discussing another vacation trip to Helen, Georgia.

Irene and Stanley had issues about faith and constancy that lasted through most of their lives. In fact, they were very similar and, had Stanley been heterosexual, they might have become attracted to one another and married each other successfully. But they both married Bob.

Bob was short. Irene and Stanley were tall.

Bob never actually divorced Irene and never actually stopped sleeping with her. He was incapable of constancy and had a compulsion to prove it. He moved in with Stanley and later had a wedding with Stanley but he was always actually married to Irene.

Picture the scene when Stanley finds this out. Worthy of a Russian novel, if it were to occur on the North American continent, it ought to be set in a mountainside inn on a snowy evening outside Montreal. Bob stumbles forward into the inn, having come from a visit to Irene, who is sick with consumption, coughing blood quietly into her bread, in a cabin in the deep mountains with snow falling in bales. Stanley receives Bob coldly and demands to know where he has been. Bob, agitated, spills the whole tale, his refusal to divorce Irene out of weakness, his act of betrayal in marrying Bob, an act merely heinous and not at all illegal since no gay marriage means spit in this country.

Bob and Stanley have a child, an African-American daughter they adopted from an unwed teenager in South Carolina. In fact only one of them is the legally adopted parent but they are understandably reluctant to admit which of them it is. Stanley dotes on his daughter, and believes she will attend Princeton or even Emory and will someday win a Rhodes Scholarship. He thinks that winning the Rhodes Scholarship would be the pinnacle of a person's life, and the culmination of any parent's dream.

Irene has a child who is not Bob's but someone else's, a child from her high school days who was put out for adoption. After years of searching, and etcetera, the child found her mother. This girl's name is Roberta and for a while she was convinced that Bob was her father and was hiding the fact from her, which made her understandably angry, though it was not, of course, true. Roberta got along well with Stanley, with whom she was certain she shared no kinship at all.

Which of these people is most likely to hurl himself or herself under a train on a wintry night near Moscow? Due to having violated the most sacred of human bonds? What indelible connection actually exists between any of these people?

Bob's parents, on their fifty-first wedding anniversary, invite Irene and Stanley to the party, and each is treated with equal intimacy, to the point that a visitor might have thought it was Irene and Stanley who were members of the family and Bob who was the outsider.

The end of the evening is the usual look through Bob's parents' wedding pictures, with the old-fashioned photographs of the old-style wedding getups, everything posed and arranged symmetrically in front of the most sacred spot known to American man, the pulpit of the Baptist Church, from which God blessed this union.

Irene and Stanley are both thinking about their weddings to Bob, and wondering why Bob's parents, in their wedding photographs, appear so much more substantial.

These more or less congenial scenes all occur before Stanley learns that Bob never actually divorced Irene. When Stanley does learn this, he becomes deeply depressed, and burns the master copy of the videotape of his own wedding, which was really only a commitment ceremony, taking place in the local Unitarian Church. Which, as everyone knows, is not a real church at all.

Were this the nineteenth century and were Stanley about

to take a long journey by train, he might consider throwing himself under the wheels after Bob's revelation. Stanley would take this step not with a conscious decision but would move toward it irrevocably moment by moment, so that even a person who knew him well, even he himself, would not understand until the very last second that he was about to put an end to himself.

But this is the twenty-first century. He could drive his car into a tree but his airbags might well save him. He might try to hurl himself under the wheels of a passenger jet as it wheeled back from the jetway, but he would probably be arrested as a potential terrorist before he ever got near those huge head-squashing tires. As for using an actual train, the Amtrak schedule through Atlanta is simply too erratic, and there is never snow.

If someone were to explain to someone else that Stanley's suicide was the result of a broken vow, the person to whom all this was being explained would simply be irritated that Stanley did not get over his little trauma and move on.

Stanley will always feel married to Bob. He has never been married to anybody else, and never will be.

Irene will always feel married to Bob. She met him when she was just a girl. He was her first—no, her second—no, her third?—true love.

Bob will never really feel married to anybody. He has never been capable of such attachment, and never will be.

Marriage is a sacred state when there is some degree of the sacred involved in its making. The legal state cannot make any such institution sacrosanct. In fact, one might argue, the legal state is obligated not to do so.

The church cannot necessarily involve the sacred in joining any two people together, either, but in the case of the church, one has to see through a good deal of hocus-pocus in order to understand this.

The end of the story is that Stanley leaves Bob eventually, gets counseling, and puts his daughter through college like a good single parent. Stanley dates and has relationships but never again undergoes a marriage-like commitment ceremony with anyone.

Bob starts to call himself bisexual and meets another woman, Betty, who insists on Bob's actually divorcing Irene. Bob marries Betty, after separating himself from the woman to whom, in the eyes of God, he will always be joined, if marriage is a sacred state.

One day Betty finds the photographs of Bob's wedding to Stanley. She thinks it's a joke at first, then she thinks it's not a joke at all. But Bob is her fourth husband, and they are getting along pretty well. So she puts away the wedding album with the photographs of the two men standing side by side, and she pretends she never saw it.

Irene, meanwhile, never marries again after Bob, and lives happily single for the rest of her life. She happens to settle on the same street in Decatur as Stanley. Now and then they stop at one another's yard to talk about their gardens, but they never talk about Bob at all.

40, 41, 42

BY ALEXANDER CHEE

WHEN I WAS THIRTEEN my father was in a car accident that left him with injuries that later took his life. On the January afternoon we expected him, a blizzard covered the state, and in the early evening my mother received the call that informed her he was in the hospital's emergency unit, in need of surgery, and that they needed her permission to operate. She gave it, and then went north alone to be with him, a family friend bringing us three children along after.

In the years that followed, she took over the family business capably, eventually selling it at a profit, raised us, buried him, fought off attempts from his family to win custody of us, and sent us to the schools we wanted to attend, allowing us to graduate loan-free. Throughout, she told me stories about him, told us all stories about him, whenever she could. And she still does. She gave me his watch, a beautiful stainless-steel Omega, given to him by his father when I was born as a present for giving him his first grandson.

Now rewrite the story: My father is gay, and my mother is a man, my other father. He and my brother, sister, and me sit at home. We are not called. No one knows to call us. My father doesn't survive his accident by three years and dies alone in the hospital that night. His family successfully wins custody of us children, the business also, as part of the estate. My other father is left out of the estate, likely unkindly, for conservative Koreans have warmed slowly at best to gay men.

I remember my father's wish was to be cremated and to have his ashes scattered in the waters off his favorite place, the ancestral birthplace of my family, a small Korean island called Narodo. His family, in particular his sister, fought this bitterly. They accused us of not knowing my father. "Cremation is for the poor," my aunt said, and it was clear to me at once he had never confided to her much of what was close to him—he would have derided such a comment. My mother conceded to burying him in Maine with a heavy heart, but at the least resisted the garish headstone his sister tried to get, which would have had a bust of him, something my father would have found insupportable or laughable. Or both. At the wake the aunt asked after the will and if there would be life insurance money, and when there was nothing for her, she pointed at the Oriental rug in the dining room.

"He would have wanted me to have that," she said.

"Alexander," my mother said. "Please help your aunt take her rug to her car." And as the gathered mourners stared in astonishment, I did exactly that.

She left at once, as my mother suspected she would, and I haven't seen her in eighteen years.

As the oldest male of the forty-first generation of my family, I am the patriarch of the next generation, the forty-second, and as such, it is my responsibility to function as the head of the family. For this, I am potentially due to receive more money on the occasion of my grandfather's passing than his daughter, my aunt, and more than almost all of my uncles. It is an ancient patriarchal tradition, common to many Korean families, and one even the ancient patriarch is tired of; he, a self-made millionaire, tired of the fighting between his children over his money, has let no one know the contents of his new will except his lawyer, and, oddly, my mother. "I wouldn't be surprised if he gave it all to charity," my mother said. My aunt had, at the time of her attempt to seek custody, spent several six-figure gifts from my grandfather, mortgaged her house twice, owed my father sixty-five thousand dollars at the time of his death and likely, if she had won custody of me, wouldn't even have kept my father's watch.

I think of this now that my sister has her first child, my first nephew. Everyone comments on how much he resembles me, and he does remind me of early pictures of myself when I was his age, wandering my grandfather's house in Seoul.

On my nephew's first birthday I spent a half hour walking behind him, my fingers outstretched for him like handlebars as he walked from flower to flower in the garden and pulled on them, saying things only he knew and turning to smile at me as he crushed petals in his fingers. I thought of my aunt and wondered if we had ever shared a moment like this that I couldn't remember, but felt strongly it could not have been the case. I knew then the specific nature of the way my mother had fought her, and when I stood with him and went back inside the house, I felt a new warmth for my mother.

"Why would I get married to Andy?" my friend Zach asked me recently over coffee. Zach is twenty-five, his boyfriend Andy, twenty-three. They are both young, beautiful, smart, and talented. As their friend I want the best things for them. One is a playwright, the other, an academic. They have been living together for a year now, during which time their relationship has deepened in a way that reassures me this is one of the things that can happen when you move in together.

"Because then you're family," I said. "Even if you never have a child, you're a family of two. Imagine that something happens to him and he's in the hospital, and that he may not live the night. Imagine that you can't go in there, to tell him how you feel, or to listen to how he feels, and it's because you're not family," I said.

He blinked. To my surprise, he was crying there in the

café. He said nothing as he collected himself, and then, "I'm going to marry that boy," he said. "I want to be in that room."

He proposed later. Andy, thrilled, accepted.

Most of what I know about marriage I learned from my family, and mostly from the marriage of my parents, who, through their interracial marriage, are a part of a generation of lovers who in some sense paved the way for gay marriage. Not so long ago, marriage rights weren't just a question of gender but also of race. It was illegal for men of Asian descent to marry Caucasian women in parts of the United States up until the 1950s, and to this day it remains controversial.

My parents married in 1964 in a church in Maine, near where my mother's family has lived for over three hundred years, and on their wedding day, both their fathers declined to attend, enraging both mothers. That my father was Korean had been something of a surprise to my grandparents, despite pictures my mother sent home from Los Angeles, where they met. Still, during his first visit to Maine to meet her parents, he won his future mother-in-law over by bringing her a present of a gold ring, charmed her little sister with his metal suitcase, and made friends with her brothers by drinking with them behind the barn. Her father was never quite won over, and I remember him as being a quiet, laconic man.

My mother had it harder. When my father left for the United States, his mother held his hands and asked that whatever he did, he shouldn't marry a blond-haired, blue-eyed American girl, which, of course, was exactly what he found when he met his downstairs neighbor in Los Angeles. His parents even sent him a wife while they were dating, attempting an arranged marriage, like theirs. He refused to meet her at the airport, and his sister brought her to the bar where my parents were on a date, by coincidence. The distraught and humiliated wife threw her glass across the bar at my father, and he rushed my mother to the door as she tried to ask who the screaming woman was with his sister.

After I was born, my father, concerned about making enough to support us, took a job with his father and moved back home to Seoul with us; my mother, in 1968 Seoul, Korea, might have been one of perhaps three blond women in the entire country at that time, and of the three, perhaps the only married one. There, she encountered the open hostility of my aunts, one of whom even set fire to the house while I was napping in it.

In the forty-first generation, the forty-second is under way: my brother is married to a German woman, and they are expecting their first child. My sister is married to a Puerto Rican man, and their first child, my nephew, so nearly the picture of me, has blond hair and his eyes are grey. Some people do ask his father whose child he is. I remember a Christmas from a few years ago when we attended a Methodist Church near my sister's in Maryland, the odd hush as our family entered—white, Amerasian, African-American, Latino—and the other families, all white, stared through their silence.

Two generations into this experiment my parents began, more and more people say, of my nephew's heritage, It's now so common, but of course, when they no longer say it is is when it will be true.

Those families in that church didn't like what they saw because it was unfamiliar. This is why I am grateful for every gay man and lesbian who went and married in San Francisco, in New Paltz, who plans to marry in Massachusetts. For each one of them I wish them long and happy lives together. Every day when I woke up to see in the paper that more people had married in San Francisco, I smiled. From where I am standing, the laws against us will not prevail. In the light of my parents' struggle and my brother's and sister's new families, I see the future of my own struggle to make my own family, all our struggles; and, for courage, I remember how in moments like the one in that church, frightening as it was to feel the collective fear of the other church members, we knew why we were there, and why we were together, and so love made us brave, as it can.

There's a picture of me holding my nephew at age four months that functions now almost like a prophecy: me, in a kitchen, holding an infant to my chest as he sleeps. Whoever I partner with in life, we will have some of this to face. While my life differs enormously from my father's, I am still his son; I face a legacy as distinct as any of the forty generations behind me or any that my mother took on when she married my father. I want for my future partner the protections my mother had, and the powers, too. I know my ability to defend myself in life, as long as I have my health and faculties. But if those are lost, I want someone to tell my stories and, as a writer, guard my legacy. Someone to rely on for the hard decisions. Someone who will keep holding my son if I can't, and make sure he grows up to be the kind of man I'd be proud of, the kind I would want as a best friend.

I don't pretend to have an argument for those who hate gays and lesbians—their idea, that our marriage rights threaten theirs, breaks my heart. I think of them, living their lives inside of that kind of logic. What other delusions do they suffer from? My job with them, as I see it, isn't so different from what my father did when he went to visit his future in-laws. Friendship diplomacy, the charm offensive: to drink with the uncles and brothers, to give the mothers presents, to make the younger sister feel stylish, all while I march and vote and sometimes, every so often, look at the sky and pray.

In *The Marriage of Likeness: Same-Sex Unions in Pre-Modern Europe,* the author, John Boswell, describes rites of union conducted in Christian churches up until the fourteenth century for couples of the same sex, and examines them to see if they were in fact marriage rites. Boswell describes the story of two Roman officers, Saints Serge and Bacchus, often invoked as the heroes of these rites, as they had taken the earliest bond of union. These soldiers kept a household together, ancient domestic partners, and were respectively first and second rank in the Roman army, and intimates of the emperor Maximian. People envious of their influence with the emperor denounced them as Christian and so they were arrested immediately and marched in the streets wearing women's clothes, and afterward again, in chains. During their first trials, they stayed cheerful because they had their faith and each other.

Bacchus was the first to die, whipped until his liver and stomach tore. Serge wept at the loss of him afterward in his cell that night, fell asleep, and Bacchus appeared to him in a dream. Dressed in his armor, he consoled him and exhorted him to stay strong in his faith. "If I have been taken from you in body," he said, "I am still with you in the bond of union . . . Hurry then, brother, through beautiful and perfect confession to pursue and obtain me, when finishing the course. For the crown of justice for me is with you."

The next day, Serge was given boots with nails in the soles and forced to walk for ten miles. The night visit had made him strong in the face of his pain and confounded his torturers. An angel appeared in his cell that night and healed his wounds, and when he faced his enemies again, they marched him again in the nail boots. When he showed neither fear nor pain, angered by what they felt was sorcery, they beheaded him.

When I read Bacchus's words to Serge, I think of Bacchus watching his beloved from one of those clouds used in *New Yorker* cartoons to show someone in Heaven. I see him watching the torture of his beloved. And then angels take him down to where the dreams of his spouse float and they open the door and push him inside. Tell him, they would say. Go on.

He wanted to be in that room.

• • •

AT ONE TIME, Christianity was the faith of slaves and prisoners, and its practitioners were outside the law of the land. At one time, Christians married friends for love alone, in ceremonies where each held a candle, each a hand on the cross, and they were exhorted to true love, fidelity, and faith. At one time, this faith acknowledged what each of us can know, at times: that love can make a hero out of you. Whether or not they were lovers, something some scholars argue over as well, these men who kept the same household had a bond that cannot easily be replicated by us today. That some members of this church would look kindly on the efforts of the state to keep us from marrying now has its own irony since, in Roman times, they would have officiated for us.

When I discovered Boswell's book in the summer of 1999, I imagined myself holding the candle, hearing the exhortation for the two of us to kiss, for God to keep me and my beloved healthy and free of temptation. I had been going to regular yoga classes, studying chanting, attending a Unitarian Church on the East Side of Manhattan, volunteering there in the homeless kitchen. I had been a direct-action AIDS activist as well as an activist for GLBT rights. I felt like I knew Serge and

Bacchus, understood how a heritage had been kept from me, much less a right. A whole idea of myself, as someone tied to a tradition, appeared. It was not so different from the way I felt when I understood the depth of my families' heritages — on my mother's side, to the first settlers of the Massachusetts Territory; on my father's, to the Chinese general who went to Seoul seven hundred years ago to meet his bride.

What I know of rites in this culture is that they do their work: Funerals let me lay my grief down. Birthdays let me celebrate being alive. Graduations tell me I've reached a new level of my life's journey. Weddings tell me love can make me brave enough to remake my family under my guardianship. Weddings tell me to be there, in that bed, at that table, picking him up at the airport, smiling at him from across the room at parties, in that room, if the worst should happen, and at that grave. And if we have children, when they ask about him, I will tell them everything I remember. I will describe the moment when he got that watch that sits now on their wrist, and how much he loved it. How he wanted it to be theirs.

Now that my brother and sister have both married, our

family has a tradition for our weddings; the fantasy began on a trip to Korea, where I had imagined being married in the style of the Korean kings, with rose garlands in the eaves. It is now more elaborate: I will likely wear a tuxedo with a long tie. The ceremony will be, like theirs, in Maine, and either in the Cape Elizabeth Church near my father's grave, or on Great Diamond Island, off the coast of Portland. There's a site I remember on that island, near the beach, with a view of the sea and surrounded by a stand of birch trees. I'd like there to be the bond of union from the book, said probably by my favorite Unitarian minister, and perhaps the belt Boswell describes in one rite, slipped around us both as we say the vows. On the invitations, the image of those saints. The wedding rehearsal dinner will be on House Island, at the lobster-bake house run by Hilda Doolittle, the island's owner and an old family friend. She had asked, at my brother's wedding, when I thought I might be doing this.

I am not the only one who can see it, in other words.

I can tie rose garlands to the trees.

Holding My Breath:
A Family History

BY WENDY MCCLURE

JO LEE WAS A NAME in my bedtime prayer; I knew that much when I was very young.

I had learned to recite the "Now I Lay Me Down to Sleep" verse, which in my family was followed by the names of loved ones to be blessed—an ordered list, like credits at the end of a movie. I sort of understood that all these people were part of a story that was too big for me to hear all at once. God Bless: Mommy, Daddy, Grandma, Grandpa, Uncle Tom, Aunt Janet, Grandma Aldona and Grandpa Mac, then Jo Lee. Then Fairbanks, my grandparents' dog. Jo Lee was my mother's sister. For some reason she was never called aunt, and for years I wasn't quite sure if she *was* an aunt. She lived far away.

• • •

THE CHILDREN'S BOOK publisher I work for did a picture book a few years ago called *My Two Uncles*. It's a very sweet book. The illustrations are in colored pencil and watercolor; the characters are full-faced and rendered in a gentle but straightforward style. In it a little girl tells the story of her two uncles—young men with nice smiles and polo shirts. Only one of them is her real uncle, the girl explains. She and her parents and her grandparents and her Uncle Ned and Uncle Phil all live in the same town, in solid old houses with big front porches; everyone loves each other. Grampy still needs to come around, of course—he can't do more than wave to Uncle Phil in the car—but otherwise things are pretty damn peachy.

The little girl understands completely. In this book it seems all anyone needs to do is understand completely.

IN PICTURES JO LEE didn't look like my mother, as far as I could tell. In some photos she looked a little like the neighbor girls who baby-sat me (Alannah and Mary Ann, who occasionally made it into the very end of my prayer). She was young: for years I thought she was always nineteen. She couldn't have been still nineteen by the time I started looking at her picture in our photo album, but it said *Jo Lee, 19* in pencil on the fat white lip of the Polaroid photo.

On the same page of the photo album there was another picture of another girl, standing against a window. I had to ask who she was. My mom said it was Susan: Susan was Jo Lee's friend. I thought *friend* as in the kind of friends I had at school. It felt odd enough to have one of them over at my house for lunch—the formality of the extra place setting, of hearing my parents call them by name. So I wondered how it was Jo Lee's friend had come to be in among our family pictures. She seemed caught there by accident. The window light behind her closed in around her hair, and her face was dark; the picture seemed to be less about her than where she happened to be.

Jo Lee lived in New Orleans then. One time, when I was four, she came to visit us in Chicago and she brought beads—a huge slippery pile of plastic Mardi Gras necklaces that I hung on my arms and put around my neck and wore around my head like a princess. I wondered where she came from.

DEAR ABBY, begins a letter my Grandma Aldona wrote in 1978. *You and your experts are wrong regarding homosexuality. They are not born. They are "made" by other homosexuals—seduced, if you will, because they cannot procreate themselves. I am a heartbroken mother of a lesbian. She was a heterosexual—I know this for a fact. I think your "experts" were homosexuals if they gave you the advice that they did. My daughter is now twenty-six years old, perhaps too old to give up this hopeless style of perversion, but my prayers are daily and relentless.*

MY GRANDMA ALDONA's outfits were as frilly and elaborate as boudoirs. She liked blouses with floppy peasant ruffles or else globs of lace at the collar. Her look appeared to combine elements of Mexican folk dance and high drag. She wore amazing quantities of silver and turquoise jewelry; her hair was tall and dyed bright auburn, even when she was in her sixties. All her makeup had ghostly, iridescent tones so that in person she looked dewy; in photos, oddly indistinct, sort of radioactive and beautiful in her own way.

She went to Mass every day, and wrote her letters—typed, single-spaced letters on legal-length paper; letters with enumerated sections, with frequent addendums and corrections in the margins. In addition to Dear Abby she wrote to politicians; she wrote supportive letters to Jesse Helms. She wrote to archbishops and to priests and a nun who had her own TV network. She also wrote to my mom and Jo Lee, whole lists of Where She May Have Gone Wrong in raising them, and detailed documentation of the slights they committed against her, intentionally or otherwise.

She kept everything in folders—dozens of files of carbon copies and drafts and letters received; we went through them after she passed away. She had a folder labeled *Homosexuality*: it was over an inch thick and it was filled with articles, with clippings from religious publications, with brochures from organizations which offered "therapy," or cures. Jo Lee has kept it. There were also folders on *Sex Education* and *Abortion*. Grandma Aldona had issues.

IN THE PICTURES from my parents' wedding, Jo Lee is wearing a dress with a big bell-shaped skirt and a pillbox hat with a short little veil tucked into it. The photo was not in color so the dress looked white.

"Did Jo Lee get married too?" I asked my mom once, when I was about eight.

"She was a bridesmaid," my mother explained.

I could tell that was the next best thing.

"How old was she?" I asked. Fourteen, my mom told me. That was even better. It was an attainable age; in not too many years I could be that old and wear an almost-bride dress for someone else's wedding—a female someone else. I didn't have any sisters, so there was only one opportunity I could think of.

"Will I be a bridesmaid when Jo Lee gets married?"

"Don't hold your breath," my mom said.

JO LEE WAS where half my Barbies came from. At some point in my childhood I'd been given her old doll collection from the early '60s. Undressed, they looked pale and hard next to the sienna rubber legs of my twin Malibu Barbies. They'd come with better stuff though: bouffant wigs and sleek gold-lamé strapless dresses—they had *cocktail dresses,* these Barbies. There were two dolls with molded hair; they often wore their bouffant wigs backward, because I didn't know how they were supposed to look. A third doll had long, slightly ratty brown hair, and the word *Midge* was embossed on her right buttock. Midge was Barbie's friend, my mother told me. (I hadn't considered that at all.)

After my mom told me Jo Lee was gay, it was hard to imagine she'd ever played with these dolls. I assumed their accessory-strewn lady ways had had no effect on her.

Then again, I was the one who lost nearly everything save

the Barbies themselves. In the course of my reckless hetero childhood, I'd broken the furniture and ruined the clothes; tiny single high-heel shoes rattled around in a can with dried Play-Doh.

Grandma Aldona used to itemize the things she didn't want Jo Lee to inherit—the Mayor of London tea set; the cloisonné lamps. "I don't want them going to the Gays," she'd say, as if that was an unspeakable fate for antiques.

As for me, I look up vintage Barbies in toy collectors' guides sometimes and sadly consider the heritage I squandered as a result of my lifestyle.

WHEN I WAS ELEVEN, my brother and I flew out to Albuquerque to visit Grandma Aldona and Grandpa Mac. *They're my only grandchildren,* my grandmother had said in a letter to my mom. *You haven't let them get to know me.*

We stayed in my grandparents' ranch house, nestled in a cul-de-sac somewhere in a bright, nearly treeless development. We also spent time with the Scanlons, a family they'd met through their church. The Scanlons had five children and a house with white carpeting. I remember a Jessica and a Michelle and a Brian and—I think—a Craig. They had shared boys' and girls' bedrooms, the way kids did on TV. Reportedly, Jessica sang, and she had a small part in a local movie. I liked them, for the most part.

We went to see the re-release of *Star Wars* with them. "Your grandma is like family to us," one of the older girls, Michelle, told me. "You're so lucky she's your grandma." I felt an odd flutter of guilt.

My mom had left the church, Jo Lee was gay, and me, *I read Judy Blume books.* I knew there were worse things than possessing a library copy of *Deenie* but I also knew, from the look on my grandmother's face, that I was going to be getting things wrong with her from now on.

JO LEE HAD MOVED back to New Mexico with a woman named Casey and later that week my grandparents took us to meet them at a restaurant. I knew Casey was a friend the way Susan in the photo was a friend. I didn't quite know whether it was okay to talk to her. In the years they were together I saw them only a few times and each time I couldn't help but think about how my family never exchanged Christmas presents with them. It was by Jo Lee's request; money was always tight.

"We met the Scanlons," I told Jo Lee at the restaurant.

"Oh yeah? Who are they?" she asked.

My mother's childhood stories and Jo Lee's are like money in different currencies; they refer to the same things but they're hard to combine, they're separate accounts. They were born ten years apart; two children in a military family. My grandfather was in the army, and they lived in dozens of places—Kansas, Maryland, California, Germany, New Mexico. The divides in time and space make the history of their family fall apart into so many segments, into this anecdote and that.

During one of the many moves, my mother says, the back

of the station wagon was piled with mattresses and she and Jo Lee rode back there—sort of recklessly, since Jo Lee was still a baby. They went through Kansas this way for hours; at some point, though, my mother realized that Jo Lee was missing. The car pulled over and stopped; my grandparents pulled out suitcases, pillows, everything they could.

They found Jo Lee had slipped, face up, deep into the crevasse between two mattresses. She was wedged there and she slept gripping her bottle with her feet. She doesn't remember this, of course.

When Jo Lee was a freshman in high school, a girl she knew told her, "my cousin is coming to visit, and he's staying with my sister in her room."

"That's nice," Jo Lee said. She wasn't sure what this girl's point was.

"Do you know why he can share a bed with my sister even though he's a boy?" No idea, Jo Lee thought, but the girl went on. "It's because he's a homosexual. He doesn't want to be with girls."

It was the first time Jo Lee knew what *homosexual* meant and it was the most unremarkable thing she'd ever heard.

It seems Jo Lee is never terribly surprised in any of the stories she tells and yet she's most often the surprise element in the story of our family.

"So why didn't we all go to Jo Lee and Karla's commitment ceremony?" I ask my mom over the phone. "You went, right? It was in 1995?"

"No, I couldn't make it," my mom says. "I wanted to go, but I couldn't afford the trip." She'd just been out there a few months before, for Jo Lee's nursing school graduation.

I want to be a little outraged about this. *None* of us went? Why the hell not?

When I was sixteen I visited Albuquerque on my first and only solo visit. My grandparents took me to the one mall I knew from previous trips; the one or two restaurants; the pool at the officer's club. They went to another church now, one where every Mass was in Latin. They didn't mention the Scanlons.

My grandfather would drive me in their Oldsmobile and we barely spoke. The whole town seemed to consist of subdivisions and expressway ramps, and I didn't really know where I was at all. I'd say "Oh, I know this street," when I thought I recognized something—a restaurant sign with a cowboy boot on it; the logo for a chain of gas stations that I never saw at home. "We've been here before, right?" I'd ask. Once, I thought I saw the movie theater where I'd seen *Star Wars.*

All I knew for sure was that there were mountains along one edge of the city. My mom said that Jo Lee lived up near the mountains with Casey. My grandparents never took me up there, though. I figured they were much farther off than they looked.

With my grandmother's permission Jo Lee came down once during my visit, to take me out to lunch and shopping.

"Are you, you know, doing okay?" she asked me at the restaurant. "With Grandma?"

The day before I'd argued with my grandmother over things I'd learned in my tenth-grade health class. She'd gone off to rifle through her file boxes and came back with a smudged brochure, which she made me read. It said:

"Contrary to popular belief, the Pill is an abortifacient. It kills embryos." After that she wouldn't talk to me until after she'd come back from Mass.

"Yeah," I said. "I know how it is. It's fine." My mother had warned me about Grandma Aldona, but I'd thought by coming to visit I could fix our family a little. I wasn't doing a very good job.

THE MIDGE DOLL I inherited from Jo Lee did not mix all that well with her late '70s Barbie counterparts. They had big blond manes, beaming smiles, starry disco glints in their eyes; Midge, on the other hand, had a voguish pout that made her look disaffected. She couldn't compete when it came to fresh-faced prettiness, but her noir looks made her the perfect foil to my Ballerina Barbie, who had a little gold plastic crown permanently attached to her head and thus could be easily cast as Barbie Prom Queen, or, if you impaled a Kleenex on her crown, Barbie Bride.

In my doll narratives Midge (or Olga, as I chose to call her) was always trouble. She plotted to send Barbie to her death by pushing her down a mine shaft (our house had a laundry chute); she crashed Barbie's parties; she kicked the other dolls around with her legs scissored out into righteous arabesques.

It probably goes without saying that most of this drama took place in the twilight of my Barbie years. I kept the whole ensemble under my bed and brought them out only for old times' sake or when someone younger came over. I was maybe twelve.

"Where'd you get *her?*" I remember someone, my neighbor Suzie I think, asking me when she saw Midge/Olga.

"My aunt," I said. By then I was calling Jo Lee that. "My *lesbian* aunt," I used to say to people sometimes.

THESE ARE TWO STORIES that I've heard only secondhand, but they're my favorite stories about Jo Lee because they're about telling off my grandparents.

1. Jo Lee was having a fight with my grandmother. In the middle of it all, she said, "Oh, Jesus, I am *not* going to take this from a person with *orange hair*." This is sort of a favorite with my mom and me. Jo Lee doesn't remember it.

2. Not too long after Jo Lee had broken up with Casey, my grandfather called her up one Sunday and insisted she come down and meet him that same day to discuss something. He wouldn't tell her what over the phone.

His urgent question was this: Was she going to go back to dating men? Now that she was no longer with that woman, had she reconsidered? This was another failed relationship, he pointed out.

Jo Lee said, "I'm forty. I've had only *two* failed relationships since I was nineteen. I think that's pretty damn good. And you know what? There's no chance I am ever going to have a relationship with a man again, though if I did, I sure as hell would have *premarital sex* with him. Be sure and TELL MOM THAT."

Not too long after that she met Karla.

• • •

I DIDN'T ATTEND Jo Lee and Karla's commitment ceremony in 1995, but it wasn't really until this past year that I made this fact into an opportunity for righteous guilt.

"You know," I'd say to friends, "If my aunt had married a man you can bet I would have been expected to fly out to New Mexico. But I didn't even *think* about how this was just as meaningful."

What I kept forgetting is that Jo Lee didn't invite extended family.

"Oh, it just kind of evolved," Jo Lee told me over the phone long-distance. "We decided to do it, and then we thought, well, let's just make it kind of a party."

Karla got on the other extension and started talking about it too. It was an intimate ceremony, about fifty people, they said. They held it in an apple orchard; Karla's father had helped set up the tables and chairs.

They'd sent an invitation to my grandparents, who didn't attend, though Jo Lee didn't expect they would. "But this was something important to me," Jo Lee explained. "I just couldn't *not* share it."

"I wish I could have been there," I told them. And I realized I meant that I wish I knew them better.

I HAVE TWO AUNTS, I like to tell people. I like the easy explanation that comes with a children's book sensibility: Two Aunts or Two Uncles or the famous Two Mommies of Heather. Sometimes I wonder how much of the charm has to do with marriage and how much is simply the symmetrical novelty of making one thing into two.

Still: to be an *aunt* or *cousin* or *parent* is to be wedded to something in nature. And then to have a partner in that, to have *another*—it makes it more like a family than an accident.

The kids in these books are so matter-of-fact about their Two Whatevers, but maybe when they get older they'll understand how inexplicably hard it is to get to Two, how sometimes things are missing—people are missing—but you have to keep counting.

• • •

I DON'T KNOW why I like their wedding photo so much. Sometimes studio portraits have that weird haze that I guess is supposed to make it look like there's so much love in the air that it forms a gentle mist that floats over every pasture at Olan Mills; Jo Lee and Karla's picture is no exception. They are both wearing tuxedos. Karla's is white. The background is just a white backdrop because you're not supposed to wonder for a second about where they are and of course you don't. Why not; they're with each other.

When my mother visited Albuquerque a couple years later Grandma Aldona spotted the photo in my mom's wallet. "Who are those boys?" she asked.

AT ONE POINT during the phone call to Jo Lee I started to go into the same speech that I had been making for months.

"Maybe I should have been there. I mean, if you had been marrying a guy . . ." And then I heard how strange that sounded. A *groom* wouldn't have made a difference in our family. We wouldn't have become the Scanlons with their nice white carpet. Our family would have figured out some other way to be a little lost and scattered and strange, to have photos we don't understand, pieces of stories that don't always fit together or in the proper order; names slipping in and out of stories and prayer blessings and wills.

Karla and Jo Lee had been dating for only a few weeks when they knew they'd get married. Karla told me the story over the phone. They were lying together in the awful narrow bed Jo Lee slept on while she stayed with friends; she was getting back on her feet. I don't know the whole story but my mom told me once that Jo Lee lost almost everything when she moved down from the mountains.

Karla said, "I'm going to marry you someday."

Jo Lee had said, "Yeah right." Nobody had ever said *marry* to her before.

Jo Lee told me she thought, *well, if she wants to marry me, I'm going to let her do it*. "In a way it was kind of selfish," she said. "I didn't want to lose her."

It sounded funny to hear her say that. I hadn't thought of it as a matter of someone else besides her being lost.

I'm straight and all, but when I heard that, I wished Karla could marry me, too.

THEY'D BEEN DATING for a few months when I met them together for the first time. They were in Iowa visiting Karla's family; it was only a slight detour to Iowa City to visit me in the tiny apartment where I lived while I attended graduate school. I hadn't seen Jo Lee in years. There had been no more visits to Albuquerque for me and I wouldn't go back until much later, when my grandparents passed away.

They came up to my apartment and walked in. I felt like I'd never seen Jo Lee before; her hair was short and she had a sleeveless shirt. Either I'd forgotten she had tattoos or she'd gotten them since the last time I saw her. I liked her faded jeans. Karla, on the other hand, wore her hair the same way a good friend of mine did, and I felt like I recognized her somehow.

They looked around my shabby kitchen. "Cute place,"

Karla said. It was just down the street from the gay bar where I loved to dance with my best friend Michael. I wasn't sure whether to tell them that.

Mostly, though, I couldn't stop looking at them. It was late afternoon in the summer and the light angled in across the couch and lit up all the dust in the air around them. *Wow,* I thought. I had the stupidest epiphany ever: *they're gay.* But it was a thought that had nothing to do with the past or my grandparents. And so it made sense like nothing else ever had.

In my head I needed to call them something. They were sitting in my living room—my aunt Jo Lee, I thought, and my other aunt Karla. That's what I called them. I mean I decided to call them family and then the story was all there.

CONTRIBUTORS

Wendy Brenner is the author of the story collections *Phone Calls from the Dead* and *Large Animals in Everyday Life*, which won the Flannery O'Connor Award. Her stories and essays have appeared in numerous magazines, including *Seventeen, Allure, Travel & Leisure, Story,* the *Oxford American, Ploughshares,* and *Mississippi Review*. She is the recipient of a National Endowment for the Arts Fellowship, a North Carolina Arts Council Fellowship, and the Henfield *Transatlantic Review* Award for her fiction. Since 1997 she has taught in the MFA program at the University of North Carolina at Wilmington.

Alexander Chee is the author of the novel *Edinburgh*. He is a recipient of a Whiting Writers' Award for 2003 and a National Endowment for the Arts Fellowship for 2004. His essays and stories are included in the anthologies *Loss within Loss, The Man I Might Become, Boys Like Us, TakeOut,* and *Men on Men* 2000. He lives in Los Angeles, California, and is at work on his next novel.

Stacey D'Erasmo is the author of the novels *A Seahorse Year* and *Tea*, which was a *New York Times* Notable Book of the Year. She was a Stegner Fellow in fiction at Stanford University, and her essays and criticism have appeared in the *New York Times Book Review*, the *New York Times Magazine*, and *Ploughshares*.

Kathleen Finneran is the author of the memoir *The Tender Land: A Family Love Story*. She has been the recipient of a Missouri Arts Council Fellowship, a Whiting Writers' Award, and a Guggenheim Fellowship. She lives in St. Louis, Missouri, where she is at work on her second memoir, *Motherhood Once Removed: On Being an Aunt*.

Jim Grimsley's first novel, *Winter Birds*, won the 1995 Sue Kaufman Prize for First Fiction from the American Academy of Arts and Letters and received a special citation from the Ernest Hemingway Foundation. His second novel, *Dream Boy*, won the American Library Association GLBT Award for Literature and was a Lambda Award finalist. His other works include *My Drowning*, *Comfort & Joy*, *Boulevard*, and *Kirith Kirin* as well as *Mr. Universe and Other Plays*, which was a Lambda finalist for drama. He is a recipient of the Lila Wallace/Reader's Digest Writers Award, and his second science fiction novel, *The Ordinary*, will be published by Tor Books. He teaches writing at Emory University in Atlanta, Georgia, and is playwright in residence at Atlanta's 7 Stages Theater and at About Face Theatre of Chicago.

David Leavitt is the author of several story collections and novels, most recently *The Body of Jonah Boyd*. He teaches in the creative writing program at the University of Florida and is writing a book on Alan Turing and the invention of the computer.

Wendy McClure grew up in Oak Park, Illinois. She is a graduate of the Iowa Writers' Workshop and her poems have appeared in literary magazines such as *VOLT, Sulfur,* and *New American Writing*. She is a founding staff writer of the acclaimed pop culture Web site Television without Pity and is a columnist and regular contributor for *BUST* magazine. She writes a popular Web log called Pound (www.poundy.com), and her memoir, *I'm Not the New Me,* will be published by Riverhead Books in 2005. Currently she works as a children's book editor and lives in Chicago.

Michael Parker is the author of three novels—*Hello Down There* (a *New York Times* Notable Book and a finalist for the PEN/Hemingway Award), *Towns without Rivers,* and *Virginia Lovers*—and a collection of stories and novellas, *The Geographical Cure* (winner of the Sir Walter Raleigh Prize). In 1996 he was chosen by *Granta Magazine* as one of the best American fiction writers under forty. His short fiction has been anthologized in the *Pushcart Prize*, *New Stories from the South*, and the *O. Henry Prize Stories* anthologies. He is the recipient of a National Endowment for the Arts Fellowship and a North Carolina Arts Council Fellowship. He teaches in the MFA creative writing program at University of North Carolina at Greensboro.

Francine Prose is the author of many books, including the novel *Blue Angel*, which was nominated for a 2000 National Book Award; *After*, a novel for young adults; *Sicilian Odyssey; The Lives of the Muses; Gluttony; Hunters and Gatherers; Bigfoot Dreams; Primitive People*; two story collections; a collection of novellas; and four children's books. She is a contributing editor at *Harper's Magazine* and *Bomb* magazine and writes regularly on art for the *Wall Street Journal*. The winner of a Guggenheim Fellowship, a Fulbright Scholarship, two National Endowment for the Arts Fellowships, and a PEN Translation Prize, she has taught at the Iowa Writers' Workshop and at the Bread Loaf and Sewanee Writers Conferences. She lives in New York City.

George Saunders is the author of two short-story collections, *Pastoralia* and *CivilWarLand in Bad Decline*. *CivilWarLand in Bad*

Decline was a finalist for the 1996 PEN/Hemingway Award and was chosen by *Esquire* magazine as one of the best books of the 1990s. He is also the author of the *New York Times* best-selling children's book *The Very Persistent Gappers of Frip*, illustrated by Lane Smith. Saunders teaches in the creative writing program at Syracuse University.

Dan Savage is the editor of *The Stranger*, Seattle's largest alternative newspaper, and the award-winning author of *Skipping Towards Gomorrah* (Lambda Literary Award), *The Kid* (PEN/West Award), and *Savage Love*, a collection of his sex advice columns. His work has appeared on the op-ed pages of the *New York Times*, in the *New York Times Magazine*, *Travel & Leisure*, *Rolling Stone*, *Nest*, Salon.com, and other publications. He lives in Seattle with his boyfriend and their six-year-old son. He is currently at work on a book about multigenerational households.